CAMBRIDGE LIBRARY COLLECTION

Books of enduring scholarly value

Religion

For centuries, scripture and theology were the focus of prodigious amounts of scholarship and publishing, dominated in the English-speaking world by the work of Protestant Christians. Enlightenment philosophy and science, anthropology, ethnology and the colonial experience all brought new perspectives, lively debates and heated controversies to the study of religion and its role in the world, many of which continue to this day. This series explores the editing and interpretation of religious texts, the history of religious ideas and institutions, and not least the encounter between religion and science.

Evolution and Religion

Henry Ward Beecher, a nineteenth-century American Congregationalist pastor and journal editor, was a renowned public speaker active in campaigns against slavery and for social reform. He was an advocate of the theory of evolution and firmly believed that Christianity should adapt itself in the face of change. Volume 1 of Evolution and Religion (published in two volumes in 1885, two years before his death) is a compilation of his lectures defending the science of evolution. In them, he discusses the implications of the 'new' evolutionary philosophy for various key Christian doctrines such as the divine nature, human sinfulness, the inspiration of the Bible, and divine providence, and asserts that change will only help and not hinder religious thought. Beecher's charisma, enthusiasm and flamboyant oratory is evident even in print, and this book stands as a lasting testimony to this influential activist and thinker.

T0382055

Cambridge University Press has long been a pioneer in the reissuing of out-of-print titles from its own backlist, producing digital reprints of books that are still sought after by scholars and students but could not be reprinted economically using traditional technology. The Cambridge Library Collection extends this activity to a wider range of books which are still of importance to researchers and professionals, either for the source material they contain, or as landmarks in the history of their academic discipline.

Drawing from the world-renowned collections in the Cambridge University Library, and guided by the advice of experts in each subject area, Cambridge University Press is using state-of-the-art scanning machines in its own Printing House to capture the content of each book selected for inclusion. The files are processed to give a consistently clear, crisp image, and the books finished to the high quality standard for which the Press is recognised around the world. The latest print-on-demand technology ensures that the books will remain available indefinitely, and that orders for single or multiple copies can quickly be supplied.

The Cambridge Library Collection will bring back to life books of enduring scholarly value across a wide range of disciplines in the humanities and social sciences and in science and technology.

Evolution and Religion

VOLUME 1: EIGHT SERMONS DISCUSSING
THE BEARINGS OF THE EVOLUTIONARY
PHILOSOPHY ON THE FUNDAMENTAL DOC-
TRINES OF EVANGELICAL CHRISTIANITY

HENRY WARD BEECHER

CAMBRIDGE
UNIVERSITY PRESS

CAMBRIDGE UNIVERSITY PRESS

Cambridge New York Melbourne Madrid Cape Town Singapore São Paolo Delhi

Published in the United States of America by Cambridge University Press, New York

www.cambridge.org
Information on this title: www.cambridge.org/9781108000208

© in this compilation Cambridge University Press 2009

This edition first published 1885
This digitally printed version 2009

ISBN 978-1-108-00020-8

EVOLUTION and RELIGION.

PART I.

EIGHT SERMONS,

DISCUSSING THE BEARINGS OF THE EVOLUTIONARY PHILOS-
OPHY ON THE FUNDAMENTAL DOCTRINES OF
EVANGELICAL CHRISTIANITY.

BY

HENRY WARD BEECHER.

LONDON: JAMES CLARKE & CO., FLEET STREET.
NEW YORK:
FORDS, HOWARD, & HULBERT.
1885.

CONTENTS.

PREFACE.

THE universal physical fact of evolution, which a widely
accepted philosophy of our day postulates as a theory of
the Divine method of creation, is one which so naturally
and simply fits many a puzzling lock, that it is gratefully
seized by many who seem to themselves to have been shut
out from hope and from the truth.

For myself, while finding no need of changing my idea
of the Divine personality because of new light upon His
mode of working, I have hailed the Evolutionary philosophy
with joy. Some of the applications of its principles to the
line of development I have to reject; others, though not
proven—and in the present state of scientific knowledge
perhaps not even provable—I accept as probable; but the
underlying truth, as a Law of Nature (that is, a regular
method of the divine action), I accept and use, and thank
God for it!

Slowly, and through a whole fifty years, I have been
under the influence, first obscurely, imperfectly, of the
great doctrine of Evolution. In my earliest preaching I
discerned that the kingdom of heaven is a leaven, not
only in the individual soul, but in the world; the kingdom is as a grain of mustard-seed; I was accustomed to
call my crude notion a *seminal theory* of the kingdom of God
in this world. Later I began to feel that science had struck
a larger view, and that this unfolding of seed and blade
and ear in spiritual things was but one application of a
great cosmic doctrine, which underlay God's methods
in universal creation, and was notably to be seen in the
whole development of human society and human thought.

That great truth—through patient accumulations of fact,
and marvelous intuitions of reason, and luminous exposi-
tions of philosophic relation, by men trained in observation,
in thinking, and in expression—has now become accepted
throughout the scientific world.   Certain parts of it yet are
in dispute, but substantially it is the doctrine of the scientific world.   And that it will furnish—nay, is already
bringing—to the aid of religious truth as set forth in the
life and teachings of Jesus Christ a new and powerful aid,
fully in line with other marked developments of God's
providence in this His world, I fervently believe.

The relations of this great truth to Evangelical Christianity, so as to show that the substantial points of executive doctrine are helped and not hindered by this new aspect in which we are called to view them, offer the field in
which I hope to do some work during the closing period of
my life.

During the past two years I have preached with specific
application of this inspiring principle to various practical aspects of the Christian life ; and those discourses
have been put together for issue in book form.   But, for a
few Sundays, during the early summer of this year, I
undertook to discuss the bearings of the Evolutionary
philosophy on some of the fundamental doctrines of our
religious faith,—the Divine Nature, the question of Human Sinfulness, the Inspiration of the Bible, the Divine
Providence, and correlated subjects ; that is to say, to
show what light, in my judgment, falls on those great
truths from this helpful view of God's methods.   I could
wish that my views might have been carefully written out
before delivery ; but I could not write them out.   I could
only hope for fairly accurate reports of what I might speak.
I have taken the opportunity to revise these reports before putting them in a book.   They appear in the following pages (Part I.) ; and will serve as an introduction of
the *general principles* on which the discourses of *specific
application* (Part II.) have been based ; and not only so,
but will show the main lines along which I believe the new
course of the old ship will largely be laid.

It is a familiar thought that the unbelief of to-day is the faith of to-morrow: and yet to-day always condemns the premature to-morrow. The skepticism of honest men unfolds the truth, and becomes the conviction of the after-time. The theology that is rising upon the horizon will still rise. I cannot hope that it will be the perfect theology, but it will be a regenerated one, and I think far more powerful than the old ; a theology of hope, and of love, which shall cast out fear. Nay more, it is to be a theology that will run nearer to the spirit and form of Christ's own teachings, he who found the tenderness of Divine Providence in the opening lilies of the field, and the mighty power of God's kingdom in the unfolding of germ and leaf and fruit.

HENRY WARD BEECHER.

PEEKSKILL, N. Y., September, 1885.

INTRODUCTORY.

THE SIGNS OF THE TIMES.

"When it is evening, ye say, It will be fair weather: for the sky is red. And in the morning, It will be foul weather to-day: for the sky is red and lowering. O ye hypocrites, ye can discern the face of the sky; but can ye not discern the signs of the times?"—Matthew xvi : 2, 3.

This could mean nothing unless it meant that, as the weather changes, so God's providential developments are presenting a diversified appearance from time to time. He was in the world and the world knew him not; he was among the then most religiously cultivated people, and he was developing a very much higher conception of morality and spiritual religion than theirs, and they could not understand it. They looked upon all the miracles that he wrought, the transcendent works of benevolence and of grace, as if they were in a circus, watching the athletic feats of men and animals. It was curiosity, not moral hunger; and they followed him here and there, saying, "Now give us a sign; now do some striking thing." He reproached them because they had no *spiritual instinct, by which to discern the work of God that was going on in their own time.* And that is the basis not only of this discourse but of the others that may be found in the following pages, on the subject of discerning those great developments of God's providence in this world, in and around about the sphere of religion.

PLYMOUTH CHURCH, SUNDAY MORNING, May 17, 1885.

That there is a great change going on, every man that is past forty years of age has at least a vague idea. Things are not as they were. Any church in any denomination that lives in the great thoroughfares of life is not what it was thirty, forty or fifty years ago. If it is so, it must be some church placed away in the mountains or off in the remote valleys, some kind of catacomb church, some church as well preserved as the mummies in Egypt. But the churches that live out-doors and have a free sun and free circulation of air,—it is preposterous to say that they are not changed and changing. Men are greatly alarmed about this,—just men, good men, conscientious men. Nor are we to trifle with their alarm. Yet I rejoice at that which they grieve over, and I grieve over that which they rejoice in.

For example, everybody notices that Sunday is not kept as it used to be; whether for better or for worse—a little of both, I think. The cords are not so tight. We do not begin Sunday on Saturday night any more. We do not absolutely forbid all cheerful converse on the Sabbath morning. We more than smile, we are not afraid to lay forth our hand, nor to walk forth in the communion of nature in field or garden. In various ways the Sabbath has been "popularized," as it is said; and over that some grieve. But whatever may be the change, there is this change:—the Church is not so awful as it used to be. It is larger, freer; it is more cheerful. Children are not petrified as they used to be. I used to love to go to church because I did enjoy walking down the half-mile of street and hearing birds, hearing the winds in the trees; but when I got into church I didn't dare to stir; and so I went to sleep, chiefly,— with an occasional rap of grace on my head. But the church was always cold and unsympathetic to my young nature. The old Litchfield church, mounted on that high hill and standing in the middle of the green,—a hill on which all the winds swept, and swept always from every direction, apparently—that great old shackling building, whose pulpit is now in the Brooklyn Historical Society—I can remember no single thing in my young history inside of that church that ever touched either my imagination or my heart,—except the flying in of swallows once in a while, that would come in of a summer-day when the windows were open. That was a means of grace to me. They were my humble angels. Now things are different. Children do really like to go to meeting, in many places, and I wish more of them were brought hither.

Then, too, religious doctrines are not so rigorously preached as they used to be. A sermon on fore-ordination, election, decrees, reprobation, would be a novelty in most congregations. And I venture to say that where they are yet preached it is done at times of exchange; the minister does not like to live in his own parish after he has preached a rousing sermon on those subjects.

The change in doctrine is even greater than I can speak of now; I shall have more to say on that when I take up some of the doctrines specifically and discuss them. But one thing is true: I had almost said our enemies, but our troubled friends I will say, are mourning at the decay of doctrine, the laxity of doctrine, the want of what is called discriminating doctrines. Their grief, if it is a matter of grief, is well founded. Old-fashioned doctrinal preaching has very largely gone out of use. It remains here and there, but it is not general; and it is growing less and less.

For there are many ancient dogmas which are either renounced or are falling into oblivion. The great doctrine of retribution in the future is an example ; the eternity of conscious torment of all that have not known Christ and been accepted by him, in its former savage and hideous form is almost never taught in the pulpit to-day—to the honor of religion and to the glory of God I speak it.

This growing disinclination to preach on the standard dogmas is creating a good deal of alarm; for although councils are slow to ordain or license a man who is not perpendicular on the doctrine of the eternity of future retribution, yet they are growing more and more charitable; and with a little smoothing, with a little explanation, men are being licensed by good sound orthodox councils, who, on that subject, are as far from their fathers as the east is from the west.

Then, there is in the whole subject of religion far more cheerfulness and elasticity than there used to be. It is true that the Roman Church, which has a great many things in it that we might well copy, dedicated one half of every Sunday to gloom, awe, profound submission of the soul to God in religion; but after the morning service had passed, the Church dedicated the afternoon to social life and to cheerfulness, and hilarity even. The old Puritan element did not. They locked Sunday from sunrise to sundown, and made it hard and barren for most men. Now the Protestant church life has changed. Church parlors have become popular. I believe Plymouth Church was the first in America that ever had in the building a suite of parlors, as I think it is also the first church in America that ever had flowers every Sunday on the platform; and the first church that ever had a hymn-book that gave to the people all the tunes as well as all the hymns that were to be sung. There are multitudes of such books now, but I believe "Plymouth Collection" was the pioneer. And taking the churches up and down through the land, more provision is made for social life and enjoyment, even for amusement. The whole region of Sunday-school life is raised many, many, many degrees above anything that was known in my childhood. It really is a comely and beautiful sight now to go into a Sunday-school and see how happy the children are; to see and enjoy the various festivals that are provided for them.

The clerical position too, is changed very much. When the minister walked down the street fifty years ago in New England, children ran into the back doors and hid. He was dressed like a magnate. He talked and walked like a being superior to those round about him. He had an atmosphere of authority, he was magisterial. He was ordained to feel that he was the channel by which God spoke directly to the people. God speaks through every man that tells the truth and speaks in love ; and ministers that do not either speak true or speak in love—no ordination can give them the right to speak for God. Once being ordained, it was in my boy-hood thought that the minister was a superior being. But the voice of the preacher to-day is " Men and brethren, we are men of like passions with you." They are no longer worshiped. They stand mostly just for what they are, and not for what their office is. They are elder brethren, not God's vicegerents.

Now I count these various changes as mere symptoms of greater changes that have taken place and are taking place underneath. They are merely the efflorescence, on the skin, of that which is at work in the blood of theology. I do not altogether wonder that some men fear these symp-toms ; but how much they will dread depends on their temperament, on their education, on their habits of judging. Are these changes and those from which they spring to be really feared by good men ? Are we drifting into atheism ? Are we drifting into infidelity ? Are we drifting into abso-lute worldliness that shall supplant all moral and religious impulse and worship ?

As for myself, while these symptoms, more or less exag-gerated, naturally would excite fear if not analyzed and understood—I am impressed with gratitude and with joy and with the most hopeful courage for the future on account of them. I thank God that I see these changes going on ; just as I thank God for seeing what the spring is doing out-doors to-day. God is certainly advancing the Church and the world in upward directions. These special changes, I have said, are only part of a great development which is in progress ; which springs from the very foundation of things : resulting from no single or special influence, from no par-ticular men or philosophies ; which hardly cares for help from human hands, and which cannot be hindered by human opposition. It is organic, universal, divine. If things are being taken up by the roots, it is to be transplanted into a nobler soil. It is such a movement as proceeds among the spheres. The sun does not rise for New York, it rises for every State from the Atlantic to the Pacific Ocean. It rises over every land which it illumines. There is going on a work that includes more or less directly the whole human

family. We ought to have expected it ; for the voice of the
whole Bible is the voice of one looking forward hopefully.
Substantially, the testimony of every part of the sacred scriptures, Old Testament and New, is " It doth not yet appear."
In every age prophets, martyrs, witnesses, said: " God is
unfolding greater things in the future than any that are
known." And everywhere the testimony of sacred writ is
that of expectation, of fore-looking, of hopefulness, of
courage.

We have very generally been accustomed to throw forward
to the millennium that hopefulness of the future; but we are
taught by more recent philosophies and theologies : " The
kingdom of Heaven is a seed, the smallest of all ; but when
grown,"—ah ! that growing, that unfolding ! When it has
sprouted it ceases to be a seed.   Shall nature weep because
the seed is dead ?   Except the kernel of wheat die, it cannot
live or bring forth, saith the New Testament.   And so in
every age, whatever has come as the fruits of past experience is the seed of the future, to be planted again and largely
to perish, in order that it may bring forth an advanced
condition of things.

It has been thought that in the millennium, or, as others
put it, at the Second Advent, when Christ shall come again
on earth, he then, as some seem to think by physical force,
by authority, will change things ; and the wicked shall all be
burnt up, and the righteous shall flourish.   But now we are
taught that that process of change has been going on from
the beginning, slowly, slowly ; that we are on the eve of a
day in which that development is to come much more
rapidly, and that it is to be an unfolding that is to affect
every process of human thought—our notion of dogma,
doctrine, government, laws, institutions, philosophies, theologies, everything.   These are all growing to a future
blossom and future fruit.   And of this not only are the witnesses such men as Paul, who says that now we see through
a glass darkly ; all knowledge that we have now shall at
length seem like child's play ; all teaching that we have
now shall pass away when the perfect day is come :—but
also we have that other Voice, " that hath promised, saying,

Yet once more, I shake not the earth only, but also heaven.
And this phrase *Yet once more*, signifieth the removing of
those things that are shaken, as of those things that are
made, that those things which cannot be shaken may
remain." That is, in other words, we have here set forth
the relativity of all knowledge, and the coming of things
that are not relative, but are permanent and shall be forever. This is the presage of those later stages of the evolution of the human race which we are bound to expect and
to hope for, though many of us will die without the sight.

Many admit that philosophy—human philosophy ; science—the physical sciences ; human institutions, such as
legislatures, judiciaries, laws, are subject to unfolding ;
that laws and customs naturally would change — with
climate, with nationality, and with advanced experiences
of mankind. They have learned to accept the fact that
civilization is progressive. Ecclesiastics believe that the
Church moves as a locomotive does, but does not change;
the track is laid by God's hand and no man may move it.
It is admitted that mere human inventions and devices may
grow, change and waste, but asserted that religion is a thing
perfected—a jewel fashioned in heaven, and the Church a
divine casket exactly adapted, and authoritatively chosen ;
it, and no other ! Like mathematical quantities, like arith-
metic or geometry, religion is definite, absolute and unchangeable. But daily experience contradicts this notion
Religion is simply Right Living. In both Old and New
Testaments it is called Righteousness. It begins as a seed.
It develops as a growth. It is relative to the individual
characteristics, to the age, the institutions, the whole
economy of life.

Every father and every mother knows that in the process
of bringing up their own families there is nothing that is
absolute to the little children. You cannot convey directly a large thought to a child. You are generally obliged
to convey ideas to children through fictions. In the history of the unfolding of truth in this world, God has made
it absolutely necessary that we should work by the shadows
of things, by the pictures of things. So then fables, para-

bles, so then all forms of fiction for little children, are helping them up, on, toward truths; and it is not until their older manhood that they are able to sweep away all those fictions by which they come to absolute truth.

Now if with a child that understands human language you are unable to instruct him from step to step upward except through symbols and similes and stories of various kinds, is it to be supposed that God, who is invisible and never speaks audibly to mankind, has revealed a scheme by which the human race can come instantaneously to a knowledge of the truth in such a way that their ideas of it are absolutely unchangeable?

Take, for example, some of the elements of religious truth. If there be any element that is fundamental, it is the existence of God. That that has been made known to the human family I suppose none of us doubt. It is the universal faith. But see through what stages the thought of God has passed, and is passing. Nobody here I hope doubts that there is a God—certainly not I. The belief increases upon me in volume and intensity with growing years and reflection. There is an absolute truth in that fact. But what is God? Ah, that is another thing. Different ages have been gradually unfolding, unfolding, unfolding man's idea of that. That the sun exists, has never been doubted ; but never until the spectroscope was invented and brought to bear on that orb, with photography to back it, did men really come to know what the sun is and was of itself; nor now, perfectly ; but knowledge stands at the door, and increases from year to year. And this new knowledge has not abolished the sun, nor changed its nature. Our ideas have changed, not the sun. And so of the knowledge of the existence of God. God does not change. He is what he was from the beginning, is now, and ever shall be ; but the human thought of God—that changes, and changing, purifies itself and shines brighter from age to age.

So too, the fact that men are all sinful ; alas! that is an uncontrovertible fact. No man can, believe it more profoundly than I do. But what is sin? What is the origin of sin? What is the nature of sin? The whole philosophy of that fact of sinfulness may change, and has been changing from the day when it was believed that sin was the working out of absolute corruption in the material body of a man, to this day, when it is to be discriminated from infirmities, and when it is to be understood to be the conflict going on between the base under-man and the spiritual upper-man. The doctrine of sinfulness is not to be abolished. I wish I could abolish the fact. Alas, it stains human nature through and through. We are all born under conditions in which we fall into mistakes and into infirmities; and out of infirmities into transgressions—voluntary and recognized and unrepented of. But what is the real philosophy of this great under-fact of human life? That may change, while the fact remains constant.

The reality of the Divine Providence has been the strength of men in every age of the world. God governs; affairs are not at haphazard ; affairs are not even the machine-operation of a well-devised mechanical world. In the initial stages of science, when men began to find out that God interpreted his thoughts to them by natural laws, or rather, that natural laws were the constant expressions of the divine thought and purpose, the religious-minded feared that such a view would overthrow the doctrine of Special Providence. But through a changed conception of the nature of God and of what are the expressions of the divine will, men are coming back to a belief in a general Divine Providence, and I think they will come back much nearer than that, although with manifold explanation. The doctrine of Providence stands, but men's ideas of its method and meaning will change along the line of experience and of further divine manifestation in the world.

Thus the component parts of theological systems may change, and yet religion go unharmed — nay, greatly helped. To-day men do not know what to do with their theology. It stiffens and hampers them, and wears them out by its weight. Theology may change, but it is not for the sake of obliterating religion, of taking away responsibility of conscience and faith ; it is for the sake

2

of giving these greater power. I think I may say, without having recently made examination of the fact, that
the Confession of Faith that I subscribed when I was
ordained leaves without any considerable emphasis, or
prominence, the whole marrow of the Bible, and puts in
the place of it the weavings of human philosophy. What
do I mean? As I now recollect, I do not think that the
doctrine of Love, as the very interpretation of the divine
nature and the center of all Christian life, and the aim
and end of Revelation, is anywhere set forth in that Confession of Faith so as to produce the impression on men
that Love is the central and the chief power. I make this
statement subject to correction, and I shall be very glad if
you will find it. There is a great deal in the Westminster
Confession of Faith that it would do you good to read.
There is a great deal in it that cannot be bettered. I quarrel with the Confession of Faith principally on the ground
of its presentation of the divine nature ; that, I think to
be barbaric, heinous, hideous. "God is Love" is not made
the center of the system: of that I am morally certain.

Now, systems come and systems go ; but the moral
structure of the human mind is such that it must have
religion. It must have superstition or it must have intel-
gent religion. It is just as necessary to men as reason is,
as imagination is, as hope and desire are. Religious yearn-
ing is part and parcel of the human composition. And
when you have taken down any theologic structure—if
you should take down the Roman Church and scatter its
materials ; if then one by one you should dissect all Protestant theologies and scatter them—man would be still a
religious animal, would need and be obliged to go about
and construct some religious system for himself. Love is
not dependent on creed. Reverence is not dependent on
creed. They may be helped or hindered by one or the
other, but they are inherent, they are vital to the structure
of the mind. Aspiration, fear, hope, joy, all these qualities are fundamental in the structure of the human mind.
Whatever form you may give to the philosophy of them,
that you may take away again ; but you do not take away

the foundation—that remains. Man as a religious animal, that remains ; and he must have provision made for that part of his nature, just as much as he has for any other.

So the doctrine of the Divine Presence, the divine efficient activity. The old theology had very much to do with the establishment of God's sovereignty. "He had no counsellor." That is a fact yet. He could not have, and be God. But the sovereignty of God was so stated that men felt that God took no account at all of human wishes and desires. He pleased himself. But infinite selfishness would be infinite infernality. Any doctrine that leaves the impression upon the mind of man or child that God is at liberty to consult his own pleasure and his own will and wish—is making a demoniac being and not a divine being, unless you do as Hopkins and others of that school did, give such new meanings to words as to show that divine will is coincident with gentleness and forbearance and suffering and all patience ; but then you have twisted language out of its ordinary meanings, for the sake of correcting a blundering theology.

Thus, too, the duty of reverence and worship is changed. It has hitherto been Fear that inspired Reverence. Awe is reverence and fear, in a mild, intellectual form. When I see a man drop down in the shadow of the Cathedral ; when I see a man crawling on his knees as it were, toward the altar ; I am tempted to say to myself, " Is that man worshiping a slave-driver or a father?" Yet that shadow of reverence and awe is an essential part of the human view of the Divine Being, and has its demand to make—in varying modes and intensities for different natures—upon the outward forms of worship. Nay, even the same individual in different moods will naturally crave and take the reverent and suppliant, or the joyous and filial attitude of feeling. But with the changing view of God the spirit of approaching him in worship changes too; and the tendency in our day is one of more and more joyous delight, as of children coming to a beloved father. The softer shadow of reverence, however, lingers still. I would not have one go to church with wild whoop and outcry. We do not allow it even in our

families. In the presence of age or of venerable matrons and
maidens all our children observe respectful decorum. So,
surely, would I have it in the house of God. But to darken
the windows, to bring twilight for the sake of darkening and
suppressing the feelings of men in the sanctuary, I would
not have that ; and am glad to see it passing away. People
who come to this church come with cheer and congratula-
tions, and exchange the voices of neighborhood and personal kindness and affection. Reverent and honored persons coming from other communions enter, and sitting
down look around with wonder, and say to themselves,
" Can this be a church ! Why, they are talking to each
other cheerfully." And yet, while there is a glow of
welcome, while there is a cheerfulness among us all, is
there any lack of real reverence ? When the Lord was
among the multitude, was he unwilling that children
should rush to him ? Now that Jesus is disembodied and
in his most royal nature, affluent and familiar and gentle,
do you suppose he is offended when we exercise the purest
and dearest affection in the house of God ? This is the
place for smiles. It is the place for happiness, and it does
not one single particle dim nor cloud the thought of the
All-Father. He takes unfeigned delight in happiness so
pure and simple as that. And that which I have habitually
unfolded for the more familiar understanding of it here,
for the regard and practice of this congregation, I think I
may say has become the general tendency of things throughout the land; that our Protestant worship is growing to be
more nearly the worship of faith and hope and love, and
less of rigor and of fear.

In view of these general statements of fact, which I do not
think will be doubted or denied, I remark in the first place
that if these changes belong to a systematic movement
under the providence of God, if they are stages and steps
by which we are ascending to a higher view of God and of
duty and of humanity, fear of them is vain and foolish.
Yet I do not say that a man is to be reproved for looking
very cautiously ; I do not say that ministers are to be reproved for being conservative and hesitant. It is very

easy for men who are ordained to the anonymous news-paper, who have no responsibility of any kind, to lecture a minister. And when they say that ministers ought to be bolder, and in the light and flash of science should say everything they think, or are beginning to think, or think they think, take into account this : when you bring a new book or a new man or a new doctrine or theory into the household, where the mother has six or eight sons and daughters, when you bring into the household anything that takes hold of the children, is it possible that she should not be more or less solicitous? Is there on the round earth anything that is made by God him-self so near and dear to us as the welfare of our children? The mother's heart first says, "What will be the effect of this on our children?" And it is wise ; it is a God-ordained principle in the mother's heart, to make her, I will not say suspicious of every novelty, but careful to consider it, and judge it by this standard : "What will be its educating tendency or its moral influence?"

But the minister is practically a mother in the pulpit. He is called in some lands and churches a "cure of souls ;" he has the care of them. His business is to train ; to teach, it is true, but to train as well. He has all classes : the ig-norant, the intelligent, the old, the young, the inexperienced. He has to minister to them all, and in the nature of things a doctrine capable of being well understood by men of wide sympathy and education might mislead those that have nar-rower education and comprehension ; and it is a very diffi-cult thing for a minister to preach things that are novel or not known as yet, so that there will not be danger and peril. He is to say to himself, "Now I must begin a great way back. I must familiarize them first with simple and elementary truths. Then, when they get this idea well-rooted, I can graft on to that something higher." And so, year by year, if he is in an ascending scale, he will lead his people up safely, and that is the great thing. He will lead them to a real comprehension of God. He will lead them to a real courage and trust and love of God. He will lead them to knowledge about their own minds, to a continual knowledge about the way of God in nature and society and the individual heart. The man who undertakes the spiritual care of a mixed congregation, young and old, will not be guiltless if he does not preach with a constant consideration of what will be the effect of his teaching in bringing up the little children and the middle-aged and all the community. In the first place, he must not preach new truth, that is, new to himself. It ought to ripen in his own soul. It ought not only to be ripened in his own soul, but it ought to be struck through with human sympathy. Before he begins to deal with higher and nobler relations as truth develops them, he ought to feel and see just how it may be made raiment and food for the starving, and naked, and needy of every gradation. And out of his own soul he must preach higher views and doctrines, and see to it that they are not misapprehended and not misleading men.

It is a great work. I have great respect for all the professions, but after a very considerable knowledge of the world outside of my own profession I still feel, not that ministers are any better than any other men or that their intellectual culture or operations are any higher than those of ordinary professional men, but this: the field in which a minister acts, or may act, is the widest field conceivable to the human intelligence. Two worlds: the themes the highest; the elements the purest and the sweetest; the adaptations infinite. Knowledge there must be in him of the whole constitution of the human mind so far as it has been developed. He is the father, the mother, the savior of his people. Such men cannot afford to be rash, nor headstrong, nor merely theoretic. We are food-givers, advancing just as fast as we can do it with the digestion of our children. Outside of that, in book or elsewhere, a man may go as far as he pleases, but as a minister of souls in the congregation he is to feed them so that they will grow up in the nurture and admonition of the Lord Jesus Christ.

It is not surprising, therefore, that men ordained to such high functions and under such circumstances shall be often-

times very much alarmed at changes that are taking place
which they do not quite comprehend. They have been walking in the steps of the fathers. Naturally they say, " These
are the great truths on which the people of God have fed
for generations, and which carried the Church through the
early persecutions ; which delivered the Church out of the
bondage of Romanism ; which stood by the great Protestant professors, when men were persecuted, driven out for
their lives ; which comforted them in the cave and in the
wilderness; which God has blessed for revivals of religion."
And I do not wonder that men having this training, and
honestly having also such retrospects, are afraid of what
are called new methods, new views, new theologies. But
on the other hand they have no right to cast odium on men
who as sincerely accept them. If they believe that there is
a progressive development of God's truth in this world,
if they believe that there first comes the twilight of dawn
and afterward sunrise, if they believe that it is certainly
true that Christ is illumining the world more and more by
his presence, they ought to be afraid of standing under the
rebuke of Christ when he says, " Ye discern the face of
the heavens, ye discern the changes that go on in the
atmosphere ; can ye not discern the signs of the times ?"

When, during our Civil War—now, thank God, more than
twenty years gone by—I was in London, at a breakfast of
the Congregational ministers, who almost to a man were
opposed to the North, I was called, unwittingly and unwel-
comely, to make some remark ; and the point that went
deepest and took hold strongest was this: They said to me,
" We clergymen have perhaps misunderstood the political
conditions in America, but we have had this, that and the
other influence in our way." And my statement to them was:
" Gentlemen, God has given you an ordination that you
might discern between right and wrong, and that you might
have an instant sympathy with that which is free and true
and noble ; and you were bound to have discerned the signs
of the times ; knowing that whatever may be the incidental
things, the North means liberty, and the South means
slavery." And I then chode them. I then bore down

without stint, that they had betrayed their duty, that they were blind when they should have seen, and dumb when they should have spoken ; and they answered me never a word. And I say to all those clergymen who are standing tremulous on the edge of fear in regard to the great advance that God is making to-day : " Inside and outside of his Church you are bound to be the interpreters of God's providence to his people. And while you are not to be rash, nor to make haste unduly, nor to mix dross with the pure gold, yet, on the other hand, you must be sure to meet the Lord when he comes in the air, when he moves in the providences of the world, when he is at work in natural laws, when he is living in philosophical atmospheres, when he is shining in great scientific disclosures, when he is teaching the human consciousness all around ; you are bound, because you are ministers of his Word, to meet the Lord, to welcome him, to accept him in all the new garments that he wears, and to see that the habiliments of Christ grow brighter and brighter, and nobler and nobler, from age to age, as he puts on righteousness and comes in all the glory of his kingdom towards us."

And to you, my people, let me say: I shall not be with you forever. I should fail to see the signs of advancing age if I did not know that within a few years another voice will instruct you.

You, young men, and you, maidens, are living in the morning which thousands of nobler natures than you desired to see, and died without the sight. You are beginning your life at a period when the disclosures of divine love will set aside the mists and darkness of days gone by. Do not pervert your opportunities, but reverently, conscientiously, earnestly accept the glowing, growing truths, and work out in yourselves a higher standard of duty, a nobler aspiration, a diviner manhood. Arouse your spiritual instincts, and at the call of the Divine Teacher awake to discern the signs of the times, and to see in the face of the sky the promise of God's coming day.

I.

EVOLUTION IN HUMAN CONSCIOUS-NESS OF THE IDEA OF GOD.

"And this is life eternal, that they might know thee, the only true God, and Jesus Christ, whom thou hast sent."—John xvii : 3.
"But grow in grace, and in the knowledge of our Lord and Saviour Jesus Christ."—II. Pet. iii : 18.

Eternal life, through the knowledge of God, as made known in Jesus Christ—is there anything beyond that in the aspiration of devout and earnest men? God-likeness and immortality—what have all the world to offer higher, nobler than that? To know God—can it be done? The very questions which excite the thinking world to-day more than ever (and they have always lingered in the atmosphere of thought) are of such a nature as this: Is there a God, personal, creative, sustaining, governing? If yes, then is it possible for the human mind to prove his existence? Can we do more than hope and dream; can we *know ?* If there be a God, is it possible for the limited intelligence of man to understand his nature or his disposition?

To all these I reply: The holy Scriptures teach that there is a personal, conscious, intelligent God ; that while the scope of his whole nature does lie beyond the reach of the human mind, yet enough of the divine will and disposition may be known to constitute a ground and reason for adoration, love, and obedience to his will, whether that will be made known by the natural and material world, or by the moral experiences of man in society.

PREACHED AT PLYMOUTH CHURCH, SUNDAY MORNING, May 24, 1885. LESSON: Acts xvii : 16-33.

In this discourse I pass by the question of the nature—
if I may so say, the structural idea—of God, and shall consider how mankind may come to the knowledge of God by
growth in grace. It is simply an exposition of the truth
that the knowledge of God is to be derived chiefly from
the moral experiences and the moral intuitions of mankind—evolution in moral experiences, as the ground and
reason of evolution in the knowledge of God.

We cannot understand God by mere enunciation; knowledge cannot fall upon us as the rain falls upon plants, nor
as the light falls upon visible things of creation. The elemental qualities of the divine disposition must be evolved in
us first, and the application to the divine nature is gradually
unfolded to us afterwards. I suspect that men at large suppose that God made himself known to mankind simply by
declaring to them what he was; that it was enough for God
to say, "I am eternal, I am all-powerful, I am holy, I am wise,
I am just, I am good." But I shall show that it was impossible that any such thing as that could take place; for although
there were, and abundantly, the enunciations of God's disposition, will, and purpose, they were made afterwards,
and in consequence of a foregoing experience in the human mind, which enabled men to understand him when he
spoke. It is true that he explicitly declared his will and
disposition to mankind, but only after mankind had by
unfolding and development made it possible for them to
understand the divine enunciation. Just as universal literature is dependent upon the alphabet, each letter of which
is nothing in itself but when combined with others spells
out all knowledge and all wisdom, so all moral elements
are dependent upon a certain alphabet; and that alphabet
consists of the faculties of the human soul and their experiences. It is by the combinations of them that men come to
any true knowledge of things spiritual and divine.

The question of the origin of man is, in many respects,
yet uncertain and debatable. It is by no means proved that
he was evolved from the inferior mammalian world, though
many positively believe it. Whatever analogies and probabilities there may be—and there are many and cogent—there

is, as yet, no demonstration of it, nor anything that looks like
absolute proof; nor do I see yet how any bridge can be constructed over the abyss between man and his ancestors, if
such there were, in the animal inferior kingdom, which shall
lead us to an absolute certainty. But that the human race
began at a very low point, as compared with civilized men,
there can scarcely be a doubt. That there is a difference
between savage and barbaric races in aptitude, in the capacity of variation or evolution, and that the human kind
entered the world not at the top of perfection in a golden
age, but at the very bottom, in an age of clay and stone, can
be hardly doubted by any one who has made himself
acquainted with modern scientific research. It is not necessary, therefore, that we should push the origin of the race
below the line of mammals. There is no reason why it
should not go there if it be so; but we do not need at present to assume that view of the matter. It is safe to say
that so far as primitive men were concerned they entered
life in the lowest savage or barbaric conditions. It is almost an absolute and demonstrable certainty that the
human race appeared on the earth ages before the period
usually assumed by the common chronology. The creation
of the world, according to church chronology, was but a
little over six thousand years ago. Scholars differ among
themselves in their calculations. It is only a calculation,
and largely but a guess, not at all a certainty. Chronology,
based upon the sacred Scriptures, is acknowledged by the
very men who make it to be uncertain; but from six to
eight thousand years, at most, has been given hitherto.
Now it is hardly any longer a matter of doubt among
Christian scientists that man made his appearance many
ages before any such chronological date as the church
fixes it at. Compared with the testimony now borne by
geology, the six or eight thousand years dwindles into insig-
nificance—six thousand years hardly amount to a comma, in
the revelation of the rocks. Incomputable ages have elapsed
since man made his appearance on earth. Thousands and
thousands of ages rolled away while men were learning the
simplest industries; ignorant of metals, fashioning tools of

stone, coarse potteries of clay, and architecture rude as that of the beaver. It is believed to have been tens of thousands of years in which men were increasing on the earth before there was any account of their occupations, of their laws, of their institutions, and of their development, whether in the art of living, or in general knowledge, or in morality. There is a vast and unillumined desert in remote antiquity where the races of this world were developing themselves before real history turns its eyes upon them. The importance of this history lies in the fact that in the primary stage of existence the human race were developing in themselves those social and moral elements which would make it possible for men to understand the moral character of God. It was a period of incubation.

We know very well that it is impossible to instruct the animals below man in moral ideas, even the most intelligent of them. There is a gulf fixed between the higher knowledges of human civilization and the lower range of barbaric ideas, as wide as the gulf between the rich man in Hades and the poor man in Abraham's bosom. It is not possible to convey to an inferior being an idea of the character and emotions of the superior, unless there have been developed in the inferior the elementary forms of knowledge; that is, of that very knowledge which it is attempted to convey. You cannot make a man understand justice who has never learned to be just, nor to appreciate it in others. You cannot make a naturally filthy savage understand the beauty of order and cleanliness, until he has learned something of it. The converted heathen of South Africa are called " shirt men," because when moral feeling has so far developed in them that nakedness becomes offensive and they put on a shirt, they are considered as having started on the right road. Until then you cannot convey to them, in their native and uninstructed state, any conception such as we have of the dignity, the modesty or the beauty of clothing. Animals may, and do, understand some physical truths in common with man. There are some physical elements in which they surpass us—in strength, in vision, in rapidity; but the sphere of common understanding is a very

small sphere, and, as it were, at a step, man rises to higher
elements, even in those things which are common to him
and the most intelligent inferior animals. Men and dogs,
alike, understand food, and discriminate between one kind
and another; but the constituents of food, the combinations of food and of cooking, the chemistry of food, man
understands, and dogs do not. Man prepares it; the inferior animals bolt it without preparation. So that even
in the spheres where they come nearest alike there is a
marked superiority on the part of the human mind. Heat
and cold may be supposed to be the same for a man, or
for a horse, or an elephant, but the causes of heat and of
cold, the remedies for one or the other, and the whole
science of meteorology belong alone to man.

Still more striking is the impossibility of conveying
downward the ideas which blossom out of civilization.
Truth, fidelity, honor, purity, endurance of trials, victories
over temptation, law, custom, institutions, social obligations and immunities and refined joys—all these things
are familiar; they are almost alphabetic in civilization;
they seem almost primary truths to us; but they are actu-
ally impossible to the inferior races of men. No clarity
of statement, no simplicity of language, could convey to
a savage correct ideas of a higher civilization. That which
makes man the most noble, and society the most radiant,
and human life the most perfect, is that which is absolutely hidden from the inferior classes of men, whether in
civilized life or in savage life, so great is the difference between developed and undeveloped faculties. Nor can those
who are at the lowest point ascend to the highest, except by
a gradual unfolding. We call it "education." Our word
education—drawing forth, educing—is the equivalent of *evolution*—unrolling, evolving—which has received, now, a technical, philosophical meaning. At the root-idea they are one
and the same thing; and we know perfectly well that the
inferior and the ignorant classes cannot come to any sympathy with or knowledge of the highest experiences of
civilized Christian nations, except by the process of unfolding in themselves first. That is the condition of the

soil in which all higher knowledge must plant itself. Words have no meaning to those who have no foregoing knowledge of the thing meant.

There must be some similarity to God developed in the human consciousness before the mind can understand the inspired enunciations respecting God's character and designs. Consider the efforts of men to build up a conception of God from the physical side, under these great laws and their operation. The deification of natural law was the nearest that men came to it in the earliest endeavors to construct a divinity. Every force in nature was regarded as a separate deity. This is the philosophy of polytheism. In all their lower and earlier stages of thought, men believed that every force that was operating was not only a divine force, but a Divinity. So the whole heaven, the whole earth, the air, the water, the solid soil, the mountains, the caves, the forests, everything that lived or had force in it, were full of gods; and ten thousand creatures of the imagination besides populated the realm around about and above their heads.

Then came, among idolatrous people, the attempt to develop dispositional elements; in other words, the next step would be the clothing of gods with some attributes, dispositions, character, giving to them a line of conduct; and they did this, as every one of us must do in our knowledge of God, by transferring to him some knowledge that was before in us, whether simple or in combinations. We must make up in our imagination and reason a conception of God derived from our knowledge of certain admirable moral qualities. We are god-builders as God is our character-builder; and thus in a limited figurative sense it must be said that every man creates in himself his own notions of God.

Antiquity, and contemporaneous pagan nations yet living, have constructed their gods and their character of God by transferring that which they know in themselves to their deities: but they have constructed their deities from their animal passions. The pride, the envy, the selfishness, the cruelty, the grosser appetites, not fit even to be mentioned, were exalted and are exalted, were made and are made, to form a part of the conceptions of divinities. The savage deities could not live an hour in modern civilization, except by hiding ; and with all the wreaths of poetry about their brows the divinities of the Roman and Grecian mythology, with a few graceful exceptions, would not be permitted liberty to walk abroad in our land. The temple of the gods of antiquity could be no other than our State's prison, so utterly abominable were the gods. They were the inspirations, the transmutations, from the animal nature and the passions of men to their conception of divinity, and were wrong, not in being anthropomorphic, but in the materials selected to constitute divinity.

At length a race appeared that struck the true path— so far as we know, the one only race. For everything that constitutes superior religion we are indebted to the great Hebrew stock. This branch of the Semitic race, the Hebrew people, have given to the world the earliest and the only true conception of God. It is a little remarkable that all Christian nations hitherto have set their faces and their hatred against the people that gave to them all that they believe from Genesis to Revelations. There is not a line of the Old Testament or the New that was not evolved by that race which now men wipe their feet on— or their tongues, often filthier still. God, as known to us, was not known to antiquity—not even to Jewish antiquity. Before Sinai spoke there was elementary knowledge ; but the knowledge that was given forth out of the clouds on Sinai would be considered now as scarcely elementary, so great has been the development since. Out of the sky, at one swoop, under the inspiration of the Hebrew people, are driven swarms of vicious gods. Jehovah is proclaimed. As compared with the polytheistic gods, he is declared to be the one, sole God of all the earth. The Old Testament assertions of the unity of God have nothing whatever to do with the philosophical question of the Trinity, which came in afterwards ; for that is a question of the interior structure of the one God ; whereas the unity of God in the Old Testament was the declaration of unity in thought,

feeling and control, as contrasted with the heathenish
notion of the polytheistic gods—the swarms of imaginary
divinities.   That grand first step is really the key and the
measure of value of those chapters in Genesis which de-
scribe the stages of creation.   Modern science has dis-
owned the constructive chapters of Genesis as a fair statement of the order of creation ; but modern science has not
given up, and never will give up, the grandeur of the childlike history of creation in Genesis, consisting in this:
that contrary to all the notions of the rest of the world,
it is declared that all things in heaven and in earth were
created by one God.   It was worth the writing, or rather
the collecting, of those legends, to have got that established in an early day: *"There is but one God, Jehovah."*

Gradually great natures, gathering the moralities and
the increasing virtues of the human family through years
and through generations, learning partly by the experiments that brought mischief, partly by the observations
and the experiments that brought peace and harmony—
gradually these men learned what were the conditions by
which the individual could live at peace with himself and
be joyful, and live at peace with his fellows and be joyful
also.   It was a matter of finding out; for it is a thing to
be remarked, that nowhere in all the Scripture history is
there evidence that there was any instruction given to man
in that long and unrecorded history of the race prior to the
advent of Abraham, in regard to the most weighty and important elements of human life.

One would suppose that if a race were launched upon the
sea of time, and had to make their voyage, they might well
have been told what the nature of the ship was in which
they were sailing, what was the method of its rigging and
of its management.   What a man's body is was never
told.   Men knew that they had a mouth, and that the
mouth terminated in the stomach, and that it was right to
eat, and necessary to eat; but the nature of food, the
nature of fruit, the nature of poisons, was never made
known.   Sickness had no books written for its cure.   Men
died by thousands, with the roots underneath their very feet

that would have restored them, and no heaven opened to breathe a word of instruction. Not until within the memory, I had almost said, of this generation, did men even know that the heart was a pump, and that the blood circulated. All the ten thousand things that we are so familiar with from our childhood that we take them as if they had always been known, were absolutely unknown. There was no knowledge that the brain was the seat of intelligence. Indeed, in the Semitic literature, it is sometimes the bowels that are supposed to be the seat of thought; sometimes it is the reins or kidneys, and sometimes it is the heart. In other words, when violent excitements came upon men, the part which was agitated and nervously stirred was supposed to be the seat of intelligence or emotion. So we have our hymns singing about "When we complain, God's bowels move ;" and it is one of the most astounding things that we go on singing about blood and kidneys or reins and bowels and heart, in face of the knowledge which contradicts reality. All of these things were unknown by any direct instruction. And that which is, perhaps, the most amazing of all, is, that there should have been engrafted upon the inferior animal man that intelligence which allies him to God, out of which comes the knowledge of God, and therefore in which was given a sufficient image of God to enable a man, from his own interior self, to know something of the constituent elements of his God; while yet no knowledge whatever of the body and of the world it dwelt in should have been given to the human race for a thousand years, two thousand, five thousand, perhaps ten thousand, forty thousand—*never*, until man, groping, found it out by himself.

Of these facts there can be no question whatever— namely, that man was sent forth in this life to find out everything; that he had to find out the conditions of his physical life; that he had to find out the conditions of his social life; and that he had to go through all the unfolding experiences by which he knew what was right and what was wrong. Now we have labeled the poisons in the jars in the apothecary's shop, and in the books are given the names of things, the qualities of things ; but there was not one word of information on the face of the whole globe when men started on the voyage of the human race. It was all to be learned, and to be learned by man's finding it out himself under the inspiration of God's natural laws ; for God's great material globe and its physical laws were the only schoolmaster that He sent to instruct the human race.

Well, as it was in regard to these things, so was it in regard to the moralities and the esthetic elements of human life —the ways of peace, the ways of purity, the ways of beauty, the ways of love, the ways of self-denial. All these elemental things had to be found out in the school of trial and of experiment among men ; and so soon as they began to come to the knowledge of these they had an alphabet. That is to say, we could begin now to construct a god out of the moral elements that we knew, through human trial and experience, to be higher than humanity in its utmost extent. We composed them; and then by imagination gave them universality, infinity, omnipotence : and that we called *God.* God is that circle into which human consciousness and experience have poured all the qualities that have been proved by the human race to be admirable, above reproach, transcendent. One after the other, in all their developments, combinations, and harmonies, in all their contrasts and unities, we put all things that have been realized in power, in gentleness, in love, in forbearance, in self-denial, in suffering for others—the qualities that have made power—all these we gather together in our imagination, and put into the eternal circle, and call the result *God.* He is the sum of all the things that are excellent and most highly conceivable in the experience of humanity ; and doubtless there are many more things to be gathered ; I know not whence, known it may be to the inhabitants of other systems than the earth. But the God of our thought—your God and my God—is the resultant of all the findings-out of the human family through the intellect and the higher moral development of the race.

Thus, as I have said, gradually, great natures, gathering

the moralities and increasing virtues of the human family in any age fused them into a conception of divinity, and were inspired to do it, as God is wont to do. Great souls unconsciously attract to themselves the noblest ideas of the age, and by dramatic imagination give to them enlargement, and a body of words. They collected the already developed elements, and in some great and glorious hour God shot through them, as it were, the lightning of his own mind, until these great natures saw the principles, saw what the combination meant that had been gathered from alphabetic forms, scattered here and there and everywhere. "God spoke to us in times past, by holy men." These were the men whose nature fitted them to gather together and perceive the real length and breadth and meaning of those scattered qualities that had been slowly evolved among the separate peoples around about, which they gave forth, therefore, as authentic and definite teachings of God to men. *They were so!* The things that have been proved to be pure, just, holy, true, and good in any generation, may safely be declared to be not only divine, but constituent letters in framing an idea of divinity. But such clearer development of God's moral character must wait, at least until a portion of the human family has been unfolded in an elemental conception of these divine attributes. God's truth, and God's holiness, and God's justice, and God's love become comprehensible only when the alphabetic forms of these moral elements have been developed somewhat in man. The nature of God has to be developed to human consciousness; and the progress of that, and the progress of our knowledge of what are the constituent elements of divinity, is to go on until the fuliginous doctrine of an unending conscious torment is swept out of the great heavens, where Love shines, and where Justice hates cruelty.

We are not teaching that God himself was subject to gradual growth. We do not suppose that God grows; the idea of change and growth is inconsistent with the notion of absolute perfection; but the development of God in the thoughts of men and in his revelation to human thought is one of the striking facts in Sacred Scripture. If all that

I have said is true—and it is more true and more widely true than I have time now to make apparent—we should expect to find in the Scriptures, which occupied themselves for at least five or six thousand years in construction (for between the opening leaf and the last leaf many thousands of years rolled), if these general views are correct, we should expect to find in the thoughts of men the initial and progressive developments of the divine nature. We do. That is one of the most striking things in the Scriptures. Jehovah marched through the ages glowing with increasing light until the fullness of time had come, and the veil was rent, and God commanded the light to shine out of darkness, and it shined into our hearts to give the light of the glory of God in the face of Jesus Christ. We reach, step by step, through the earlier periods, an imperfect disclosure of God. As we advance through a thousand years, the Supreme is more comprehensibly represented to us. The grander elements are evolved, larger moral influences are made to flow through the orb of divine existence ; and through dark and twilight periods the work still goes on. The great mill was grinding the pigments that were to set forth his portraiture, and what seem like dark ages were the ages of preparation, as night is a preparation for the day, until the fullness of time when Jesus Christ was born, and that which before had been gathered up from fragmentary elements evolved from human consciousness and human experience stood before us personified in the one man—absolutely perfect in body, in health, in wisdom, in all social excellence, in all moral qualities, the one fit manifestation of God, so far as he could be made known to human intelligence. The Bible is thus a grand evolution of the nature of God. It is the unfolding of his progress, that is to say, of the progress of the human mind respecting him.

In this view let me say, next, that the petty criticisms which peck at God's word, and are amazingly contemptible in the presence of this orient light which arose in twilight but waxed brighter and brighter toward the perfect day, ought to be the marvel and the wonder of men. What if there be anachronisms in the Bible? What does that amount to? What if there should be mistakes in dates, stumblings of good men, worn-out and wasted customs still embalmed? What if there should be imperfect laws permitted? What if the dust and the detritus of wretched peoples and corrupt ages should still be found here and there in the Bible? They are but fleeting elements, and have their use in marking the stages of development by which the human intelligence rose from darkness into relative light, and the conscience from being soiled into relative purity, and a higher faith was being developed. The Bible is not a book written as John Milton wrote "Paradise Lost," nor is it a book written as a man writes a history. It is not a book ; it is a series of books, with intervals of hundreds of years between. It is the record of the progress of the human race in their development into the divine idea through the medium of right-living. It is the serial history of the construction of the noblest elements that belong to human consciousness.

Should I, if I had stood upon the Acropolis, and discovered that there were spiders in the great temple, or that there was a leak in the roof, or that there was dust settled upon the cornices, blow up the building because I saw these specks in it? Yet there are men who deride this grandest collection of the evolutions of human consciousness towards the highest ideal. They have no conception of the grandeur of this movement, nor of the grandeur of its results. God, that fills the whole heaven, and irradiates the air, and his power which fills the globe, and the steps by which he brought the majesty of his being to the consciousness of the human family—all that is nothing ! A light-house that stands upon some jutting point to throw cheer and guidance afar out over the stormed waters—is it nothing that it guides fleet after fleet safely past the peril and into the harbor? What if there is a crack in the walls, or some scratch on the glass, or if there is some other defect in the structure itself? These are petty, miserable, ungenerous, unphilosophical objections to the word of God. I would not have left out anything of the Old Testament ; for, al-

though men, by forced construction, undertake to justify
corresponding elements in our time, the old elements are,
by true reading, merely the landmarks and stages through
which mankind has come up individually and in associations to the present eminence.   The Old Testament has in
it much straw, but the wheat which grew on it is in our
garner.   Like Christ's vine, it beareth more fruit by cutting away the dead branches.   The scaffoldings by which
venerable men builded the spiritual temple are yet standing, and in the thought of many are as sacred as the temple itself.   Without them men could not have builded;
but now they hide the building of God.

We go back to look for the diseases of antiquity, and these
elements are revelatory.   There was a time when men sac-
rificed to idols.   That has gone past.   There was a time
when men, yet ignorant of the best social economics, en-
joyed (or not, as the case may have been) plurality of wives.
That has long since gone down.   There was a time when
women had no rights in the presence of their husbands, who
could abandon them at will; but when Christ came he said
that woman must rise unto the dignity of man himself.   You
shall not separate her from you merely on a whim, you
shall give her a legal dismission, and but for one cause, and
that is adultery, which violates   the   very fundamental
element that makes the woman a wife.   All these elements,
scattered up and down through the Bible, which make so
much controversy, are transcendently important when they
are put in their true relation to time and to the work recorded in the Bible; but they are not our models any more
than the shoes I wore when I was seven years old are my
models when I am seventy.

Nor has the principle upon which God has made himself
known to men yet expended its force.   There are a thousand
things that we are now asserting to-day by the force of
exalted and rectified moral consciousness.   There are
many ancient dogmas and many received theologic
doctrines that are being arrayed in vain against Christianity
and reform.   There are multitudes of mere idolaters of the
Book who say the Bible is the revelation of God, and that

it is the only revelation he has ever made. It surely contains a revelation, but not a completed revelation—God has not done revealing. The Bible contains a revelation of moral truth, through the unfolding consciousness of good men. Sometimes it was but the root that appeared, sometimes the leafy stem, sometimes the blossom; but all of these on the way to the final revelation of moral truth in the universal Christian consciousness of the Church, that is, in the highest consciousness of truth, faith and love! The spiritual moral consciousness of Christendom does not annul the early teachings of the Sacred Scriptures, but unfolds and fulfills them. Germs have become growths, truths, histories; dim truths have become distinct; buds have opened into blossoms; blossoms have changed to fruits.

Not only is the moral consciousness of Christian men a real thing, but it is indispensable, and is in strict and striking analogy with the method by which the truth of God in Jesus Christ has been made known to the world. It is reproduced in the life of every Christian—namely, this method of the development of God. Every man that begins to be a Christian, begins at the alphabetic forms. Day by day he grows in grace, and in the knowledge of the Lord and Saviour, Jesus Christ; but the grace must needs come first. It is action and reaction. All grace interprets Christ, and all knowledge of Christ acts back again to develop grace in the souls of men. Every Christian is in a process of sanctification, and his perfection comes hereafter and in heaven. The phenomenon of sanctification, the gradual progress of sanctification is the application of this great truth which interprets the very genius of the whole Scripture—namely, that men come to a higher and higher knowledge of God through their own experiences. Christ becomes manifest to them more and more through long trials. Men learning patience for themselves, come to admire the infinite long-suffering and patience of God. A self-denying love—compassion for inferiors and for the imperfect—develops a true conception of what is that wonderful love of God in Christ Jesus that saves a world of sinners. By laying down our lives, or by holding them not for our own benefit, but for those that need us, we have learned what is the power of the Lord Jesus Christ, and what is the meaning of his covenant of grace, and of his example, and of his atonement, and of the elementary form of all that constitutes what may be called the scheme of redemption. They are all of them evolved in the human kind from the incipient experiences of God's people.

Not only this: as the individual experience interprets to the individual the thing that is true of God and holiness, so the collective experiences of any generation, and among all races and classes of men, become significant of the divine thought itself. God never revealed to man anything of moral or spiritual, except through the foregoing experiences of men in regard to its moral quality. Whatever grows thus is the result of the application of the highest and the noblest truths to moral consciousness. Whatever has been true in all ages, or in the multitude of ages, and in all conceivable circumstances, becomes a moral law. The Roman Church recognizes it, and with but one objection, I agree with the Roman Church in that matter; for it teaches us that inspiration is not yet done, and revelation is not yet complete, but that God is using the Church to interpret his nature and his will. It is said that he is using the *Roman Catholic* Church to do it, and that all who are outside of it get none of the light unless they borrow it. I say that God employs the Roman Catholic Church and the Protestant Churches. He employs all of them together; with some light feebly thrown in, I think, from the more intelligent idolatrous people, and from great moral teachers—for there have been many of them in later ages— and from the average experiences of all Christian men, or those that are allied to them, as the Roman Centurion was allied to Peter and the earlier Apostles. All these elements of human experience are authoritative; and as authoritative as if they were spoken from Mount Sinai or enunciated from Mount Calvary. The age of inspiration has not perished; its sun has not set. The light is flowing in broader streams; and the resultant of any long and severe trial, of any rectified and finally approved judgment as it regards humanity, justice, purity, rectitude, based on the whole experience of the churches of God on earth, is a substantial decree of God, and a revelation of God, and an inspiration from God, and is authoritative upon the conscience and the understanding of men.

I repeat: The age of inspiration has not perished. Its sun has not set. All of revelation that has gone before is but as seed for the future. A day has come when all dogmas, doctrines, formulas, laws and governments of the Church, must be judged by the enlightened moral consciousness of the great assembly of Christ-like men, whether in church bounds or out of them. God's Word will no longer be a shackle to impede new inspirations, but wings to lift men into that luminous atmosphere thrown up by all experiences of good men from the beginning. There are higher and higher stages of knowledge and experience yet before the Christian Churches and the world—the moral consciousness of Christendom, as God's way of making himself known. The Old Testament must be lived over again, and the New Testament, and out of this soil of the human soul, so fertilized, will spring new growth, new flowers, new truths. And so the tree of knowledge blighted in Eden shall, in these later days, bring forth all manner of fruits, and its very leaves shall be for the healing of the nations. God has much to say yet to the Race. The world is not ripe. It is coming to itself in the far future.

Every development, then, of piety, every reinforcement of humanity, every development of love in strength, in breadth, in exquisite fineness, in beauty, every harmonization of the highest moral qualities, is gathering material for a clearer view of God and for a nobler humanity.

Once more: human intellect, in the scientific sense of that term, as a mere researching force, can never discover God, except so far as he is capable of material representation. Largely, in Continental Europe, scientific men stand apart from organized religion, and are either agnostic or atheistic. They simply say, "Reason cannot descry God; and therefore, as nothing can be accepted as true which has not had its probation in the school of reason, either we do not be-

lieve or we do not know." Both of these states amount to
the same thing practically—*no God.* That is their attitude
to-day; and they look down upon enthusiasm and imagination as things not to be relied upon. "It is mere emotion;
it is the phantasy of faith; it is a beautiful thing; I would
not disturb it in anybody: but it has no validity."

Now, so far as the diameter of the sun, or the structure
of the planetary system, or the chemical nature of materials,
or the history of the unfolding of the rocks and the soils of
the globe are concerned, human feeling has no authority
or function; but truths that are represented by human consciousness and affection can never be discerned by the intellect alone. Quite the contrary. While we are indebted
to the spirit of physical scientific investigation for much,
and increasingly every year, there are some spheres that are
mightier than the mere physical intellect of man. There
are those spheres that make man what he is, as distinguished
from the brutes, or from the material man. There are some
qualities efflorescent, evaporating, that rise up and reach
like the smoke of accepted sacrifices to the very presence
of God ; and in regard to those truths mathematics has
nothing to do, the laboratory has nothing to do, and instruments of measurement have nothing to do. When the
question is as to moral truth, the heart sits as chief justice,
and the reason is merely an advocate standing before its
bar. In the court, therefore, of the highest intelligence in
regard to spiritual things, man's conscience, man's faith,
man's enthusiasm are legitimate,—legitimate experiment-
ers, legitimate enunciators of the truth.

So far forth for this morning; with only one single more
point. After all this long progress and unfolding of the
human thought of God, and after all the beneficial fruits
that have been shaken down from the boughs of the tree of
knowledge, we have only the beginning of knowledge. We
are in relation to the reality that we approach, as a child is
in relation to his manhood, and to things he is going to
understand perfectly. When that which is perfect shall
come, all this fragmentary knowledge will pass away, because we shall see the whole of everything in **the clearer**

light of the other world. Now, we know in part, here a little, there a little, fragmentarily. Now, human life is like a half-finished portrait, the features marked out and hinted at, some one part perhaps carried further than another; but no man can determine what it is, or how it shall look when it is perfected. In this life we are grinding pigments, we are collecting materials; we but dimly see, and that imperfectly. But there will come a day when life and all its troubles will be past. There will come a day when I shall know even as I am known; and as God, the all-knowing, looks through and through me, and knows me altogether, I shall behold him as he is, and all shadows and partialities will have passed away forever.

THE TWO REVELATIONS.

"All things were made by Him, and without Him was not anything made that was made."—John i: 3.

That the whole world and the universe were the creation of God is the testimony of the whole Bible, both Jewish and Christian; but how he made them—whether by the direct force of a creative will or indirectly through a long series of gradual changes—the Scriptures do not declare. The grand truth is that this world was not a chance, a creative fermentation, a self-development, but that it was the product of an Intelligent Being, that the divine will in the continuance of this world manifests itself under the form of what are called natural laws, and that the operations of normal and legitimate laws are the results of divine will.

There are two records of God's creative energy. One is the record of the unfolding of *man* and of the race under the inspiration of God's nature: this is a mere sketch; of the ancient periods of man there is almost nothing known. The other of these records or revelations—if you choose to call them so—pertains to the physical globe, and reveals the divine thought through the unfolding history of *matter;* and this is the older. So we have two revelations: God's thought in the evolution of matter, and God's thought in the evolution of mind; and these are the Old Testament and the New—not in the usual sense of those terms, but in an appropriate scientific use of them.

In that great book of the Old there is a record of the

PLYMOUTH CHURCH, SUNDAY MORNING, May 31, 1885. LESSON: Psalm cxxxix.

44

progress, order, and result of God's thought in regard to
the globe as a habitation for man. Though not every stage,
yet the chief stages of preparation of this dwelling for man
have been discovered and are now being deciphered and
read. The crude, primitive material of the world of matter,
the igneous condition, the aqueous stages, the dynamic and
chemical periods, the gradual formation of the soil, the
mountain-building, the dawn of life, vegetable and animal,
the stages of their progress—are not all these things written
in the scientific revelation of God's history of creation?
When I reflect upon the range of the invisible and the silent
God, with the vast and well-nigh incomprehensible stretch
of time, and of his compassionate waiting and working
through illimitable ages and periods, compared with which
a million years as marked by the clock are but seconds;
when I reflect that the silent stones and the buried strata
contain the record of God's working, and that the globe itself is a sublime history of God as an engineer and architect
and as a master-builder, I cannot but marvel at the indifference with which good men have regarded this stupendous
revelation of the ages past, and especially at the assaults
made by Christian men upon scientific men who are bringing to light the long-hidden record of God's revelation in
the material world.

With what eagerness has the world heard of the discovery
in Egypt of the tomb that contained the buried kings of the
Pharaohnic dynasty! But what are all these mighty kings,
wrapped for three thousand years in the shroud of silence,
compared with the discovery of God's method and the results of creation millions of centuries ago, retained in the
rocks? Were the two tables of stone, written by the finger
of God, a memorial to be revered, and their contents to be
written in letters of gold in all men's churches, and yet his
ministers and priests turn with indifference or with denun-
ciation, even with scorn, sometimes, from the literature of
the rocks written by the hand of God all over the earth?
What were the Ten Commandments but a paragraph out
of the book of the divine revelation of nature? Ages before Sinai itself was upheaved in the progress of divine

world-building; ages before the human race was enough advanced to have made the Ten Commandments possible, God was slowly moulding the world that was to contain within itself its own history. Science is but the decipher-ing of God's thought as revealed in the structure of this world; it is a mere translation of God's primitive revela-tion. If to reject God's revelation of the Book is infidelity, what is it to reject God's revelation of himself in the struc-ture of the whole globe? There is as much infidelity in regard to the great history that science unfolds to-day, as there is in regard to the record of the Book—and more! The primitive prefatory revelation of the structural thought of God in preparing a dwelling for the human race—is that nothing? Man had a cradle represented to antiquity as the poetical Eden; but the globe itself had a different Eden, one of fire, convulsions, clouds and storms, of grinding ice and biting chemistry preparing the soil.

To be sure, the history of man in the Bible is more im-portant than the history of the globe. The globe was created for man as a house is created to serve the family. But both are God's revelations; both are to be received with intelli-gent reverence; both are to be united and harmonized; both are to be employed in throwing light, the one upon the other. That noble body of investigators who are decipher-ing the hieroglyphics of God inscribed upon this temple of the earth are to be honored and encouraged. As it is now, vaguely bigoted theologists, ignorant pietists, jealous churchmen, unintelligent men, whose very existence seems like a sarcasm upon creative wisdom, with leaden wit and stinging irony swarm about the adventurous surveyors who are searching God's handiwork and who have added to the realm of the knowledge of God the grandest treasures. Men pretending to be ministers of God, with all manner of grimace and shallow ridicule and witless criticism and un-productive wisdom, enact the very feats of the monkey in the attempt to prove that the monkey was not their an-cestor.

It is objected to all assertions of the validity of God's great record in matter, that science is uncertain and unripe;

that men are continually changing the lines of science, that it will not do to rest upon the results of scientific investigation. It will be time to consider science when it has ripened into a certainty, say men, but not now. Well, as the case stands, how is the record of the book any more stable and intelligible than the record of the rock? The whole Christian world for two thousand years, since the completion of the canons, has been divided up like the end of a broom into infinite splinters, quarreling with each other as to what the book did say, and what it did mean. Why then should men turn and say that scientific men are unsettled in their notions? At the congress of Christian churches in Hartford recently, the Rev. Dr. Hopkins, a prominent high-churchman, said: " No less than nineteen different varieties of Christianity are at present trying to convert the Japanese. The nineteen do not agree as to what the ministry is, nor as to the word, some including the Apocrypha, and others discarding it altogether; and many differing as to the meaning of the Scriptures. Nor are they agreed as to the Sacraments. So too on doctrine, discipline, and worship. There are all sorts of contradictions of belief. Now, if Christians, with eighteen centuries of accumulated tradition cannot agree, how can we expect the heathen to solve the great riddle?" This is not mine, but I give a hearty Amen to it, and only find fault with it because it is not strong enough. When men, therefore, attempt to pour ridicule upon the legitimate deductions of scientific investigation, that have passed through the periods of trial, discussion, and proof, as if they were less praiseworthy than the declarations of the written revelation, I say to them, "No ground can be less tenable than such a ground as yours if we will look at the way in which the written revelation is misunderstood, and into the infinite splittings and divisions which men have made in attempting to interpret what is said to be the more stable revelation of the truth."

It is said, or thought, that a layman should not meddle with that which can be judged by only scientific experts: that science demands a special training before one can discern correctly its facts, or judge wisely of the force of its conclusions. This is true; it is true both of those who accept and those who deny its results. But, when time and investigation have brought the scientific world to an agreement, and its discoveries pass into the hands of all men, there comes an important duty, which moral teachers, parents, and especially clergymen, are perhaps as well or better fitted to fulfill than mere scientists, viz., to determine what effect the discoveries of science will have upon questions of morality and religion. It is to this aspect that the best minds of the Christian ministry are now addressing themselves.

It may be well before going further to expose some popular errors regarding the Evolutionary philosophy— now so widely accepted by the scientific world—and to point out some of the changes which it will work out in the schools of theology, as a new interpreter of God's two revelations.

A vague notion exists with multitudes that science is infidel, and that Evolution in particular is revolutionary— that is, revolutionary of the doctrines of the Church. Men of such views often say, "I know that religion is true. I do not wish to hear anything that threatens to unsettle my faith." But faith that can be unsettled by the access of light and knowledge had better be unsettled. The intensity of such men's faith in their own thoughts is deemed to be safer than a larger view of God's thoughts. Others speak of Evolution as a pseudo-science teaching that man descended from monkeys, or ascended as the case may be. They have no conception of it as the history of the divine process in the building of this world. They dismiss it with jests, mostly ancient jests; or, having a smattering of fragmentary knowledge, they address victorious ridicule to audiences as ignorant as they are themselves.

Now the ascent of man from the anthropoid apes is a mere hypothesis. It has not been proved; and in the broader sense of the word "proved," I see certainly no present means of proving it. It stands in the region of hypothesis, pressed forward by a multitude of probabilities. The probabilities are so many, and the light which this hypothesis throws upon human history and human life and phenomena is such that I quite incline to the supposition that it is, in the order of nature, in analogy with all the rest of God's work, and that in the ascending scale there was a time unknown, and methods not yet discovered, in which man left behind his prior relatives, and came upon the spiritual ground which now distinguishes him from the whole brute creation. Of one thing I am certain, that whatever may have been the origin, it does not change either the destiny or the moral grandeur of man as he stands in the full light of civilization to-day. The theory of the evolution of the human race from an inferior race, not proved and yet probable, throws light upon many obscure points of doctrine and of theology that have most sadly needed light and solution.

First, then, what is Evolution, and what does it reveal? The theory of Evolution teaches that the creation of this earth was not accomplished in six days of twenty-four hours; that the divine method occupied ages and ages of immense duration; that nothing, of all the treasures of the globe as they now stand, was created at first in its present perfectness; that everything has grown through the lapse of ages into its present condition ; that the whole earth, with their development in it, was, as it were, an egg, a germ, a seed; that the forests, the fields, the shrubs, the vineyards, all grasses and flowers, all insects, fishes, and birds, all mammals of every gradation, have had a long history, and that they have come to the position in which they now stand through ages and ages of gradual change and unfolding. Also that the earth itself went through a period of long preparation, passing from ether by condensation to a visible cloud form with increasing solidity, to such a condition as now prevails in the sun ; that it condensed and became solid ; that cold congealed its vapor ; that by chemical action and by mechanical grinding of its surface by ice a soil was prepared fit for vegetation, long before it was fit for animal life ; that plants simple and coarse came first and developed through all stages of complexity to the present conditions of the vegetable kingdom ; that

4

aquatic, invertebrate animals were the earliest of animals, according to the testimony of fossils in the earth. Fishes came next in order, then amphibians, then reptiles. " All these tribes were represented by species before the earliest of the mammals appeared. The existence of birds before the earliest mammal is not proved, though believed by some paleontologists upon probable evidence. The early mammals were marsupial, like the opossum and the kangaroo, and lived in the same era called by Agassiz the reptilian period. True mammals came into geologic history in the tertiary era. Very long after the appearance of the first bird came man, the last and grandest of the series, it is doubtful whether in the tertiary period or immediately sequent. It is not established whether his bones or relics occur as far back as the tertiary era."

This is a very brief statement, not my own, but that of Professor Dana, of renown. No man is more trusted, more careful, more cautious than he, and this brief history of the unfolding series I have taken bodily from his writings.

Second.—As thus set forth, it may be said that Evolution is accepted as *the method* of creation by the whole scientific world, and that the period of controversy is passed and closed. A few venerable men yet live, with many doubts; but it may be said that ninety-nine per cent. —as has been declared by an eminent physicist—ninety-nine per cent. of scientific men and working scientists of the world are using this theory without any doubt of its validity. While the scientific world is at agreement upon this *order* of occurrence, it has been much divided as to the *causes* which have operated to bring about these results. There is a diversity of opinion still, but with every decade scientific men are drawing together to a common ground of belief.

Third.—The theory of Evolution is the *working* theory of every department of physical science all over the world. Withdraw this theory, and every department of physical research would fall back into heaps of hopelessly dislocated facts, with no more order or reason or philosophical

coherence than exists in a basket of marbles, or in the juxtaposition of the multitudinous sands of the seashore. We
should go back into chaos if we took out of the laboratories,
out of the dissecting-rooms, out of the fields of investigation, this great doctrine of Evolution.

Fourth.—This science of Evolution is taught in all advanced academies, in all colleges and universities, in all medical and surgical schools, and our children are receiving it as
they are the elements of astronomy or botany or chemistry.
That in another generation Evolution will be regarded as
uncontradictable as the Copernican system of astronomy,
or the Newtonian doctrine of gravitation, can scarcely be
doubted. Each of these passed through the same contradiction by theologians. They were charged by the Church,
as is Evolution now, with fostering materialism, infidelity,
and atheism. We know what befell Galileo for telling
the truth of God's primitive revelation. We know, or do
not know, at least, how Newton stood charged with infidelity and with atheism when he announced the doctrine
of gravitation. Who doubts the heliocentric theory to-day?
Who doubts whether it is the sun which is moving round
the earth or the earth round the sun? Who doubts that
the law of attraction, as developed by Newton, is God's
material law universally? The time is coming when the
doctrine of Evolution, or the method of God in the creation
of the world, will be just as universally accepted as either
of these great physical doctrines. The whole Church fought
them; yet they stand, conquerors.

Fifth.—Evolution is substantially held by men of profound Christian faith: by the now venerable and universally
honored scientific teacher, Professor Dana of Yale College, a devout Christian and communicant of a Congregational Church; by Professor Le Conte of the University of
California, an elder in the Presbyterian Church; by Presi-
dent McCosh of Princeton College, a Presbyterian of the
Presbyterians, and a Scotch Presbyterian at that; by
Professor Asa Gray of Harvard University, a communicant of the Christian Church; by increasing numbers of
Christian preachers in America; by Catholics like Mivart,

in England; by Wallace, a Christian not only, but of the
spiritualistic school; by the Duke of Argyle, of the Scotch
Presbyterian Church ; by Ground, an ardent admirer of
Herbert Spencer and his whole theory,though rejecting his
agnosticism—an eminent and leading divine in the Church
of England; and finally, among hundreds of other soundly
learned and Christian men, by the Bishop of London,
Dr. Williams, whose Bampton Lectures for 1884 contain a
bold, frank, and judicial estimate of Evolution, and its relations to Christianity.

Sixth.—To the fearful and the timid let me say, that
while Evolution is certain to oblige theology to reconstruct
its system, it will take nothing away from the grounds of
true religion.   It will strip off Saul's unmanageable armor
from David, to give him greater power over the giant.
Simple religion is the unfolding of the best nature of man
towards God, and man has been hindered and embittered
by the outrageous complexity of unbearable systems of
theology that have existed.   If you can change theology,
you will emancipate religion; yet men are continually con-
founding the two terms, religion and theology.   They are
not alike.   Religion is the condition of a man's nature as
toward God and toward his fellow-men.   That is religion
—love that breeds truth, love that breeds justice, love
that breeds harmonies of intimacy and intercommunication,
love that breeds duty, love that breeds conscience, love
that carries in its hand the scepter of pain, not to destroy and to torment, but to teach and to save.   Religion
is that state of mind in which a man is related by his
emotions, and through his emotions by his will and conduct, to God and to the proper performance of duty in this
world.   Theology is the philosophy of God, of divine government, and of human nature.   The philosophy of these
may be one thing; the reality of them may be another and
totally different one.   Though intimately connected, they
are not all the same.   Theology is a science; religion, an
art.

Evolution will multiply the motives and facilities of
righteousness, which was and is the design of the whole

Bible. It will not dull the executive doctrines of religion, that is, the forms of them by which an active and reviving ministry arouses men's consciences, by which they inspire faith, repentance, reformation, spiritual communion with God. Not only will those great truths be unharmed, by which men work zealously for the reformation of their fellow-men, but they will be developed to a breadth and certainty not possible in their present philosophical condition. At present the sword of the spirit is in the sheath of a false theology. Evolution, applied to religion, will influence it only as the hidden temples are restored, by removing the sands which have drifted in from the arid deserts of scholastic and medieval theologies. It will change theology, but only to bring out the simple temple of God in clearer and more beautiful lines and proportions.

Seventh.—In every view of it, I think we are to expect great practical fruit from the application of the truths that flow now from the interpretation of Evolution. It will obliterate the distinction between natural and revealed religion, both of which are the testimony of God ; one, God's testimony as to what is best for man in his social and physical relations, and the other, what is best for man in his higher spiritual nature. What is called morality will be no longer dissevered from religion. Morals bear to spirituality the same relation which the root bears to the blossom and the fruit. Hitherto a false and imperfect theology has set them in two different provinces. We have been taught that morality will not avail us, and that spirituality is the only saving element : whereas, there is no spirituality itself without morality; all true spirituality is an outgrowth, it is the blossom and fruit on the stem of morality. It is time that these distinctions were obliterated, as they will be, by the progress and application of the doctrine of Evolution.

In every view, then, it is the duty of the friends of simple and unadulterated Christianity to hail the rising light and to uncover every element of religious teaching to its wholesome beams. Old men may be charitably permitted to die in peace, but young men and men in their prime are by God's providence laid under the most solemn obligations to thus discern the signs of the times, and to make themselves acquainted with the knowledge which science is laying before them. And above all, those zealots of the pulpit—who make faces at a science which they do not understand, and who reason from prejudice to ignorance, who not only will not lead their people, but hold up to scorn those who strive to take off the burden of ignorance from their shoulders—these men are bound.to open their eyes and see God's sun shining in the heavens.

That Evolution applied will greatly change the reading and the construction of the earlier periods of the Scripture history cannot be doubted. The Bible itself is one of the most remarkable monuments of the truth of the evolutionary process. There has been an immense amount of modern ignorance imported into the Bible. Again the Lord is turning out the money-changers, and those who sell oxen and doves, from the temple. But that operation of old left the temple cleansed and pure for religious uses. With many thoughtful Christian men, large tracts of the Bible lie uncultivated and unused. They do not use the whole; yet if any should take out a single text there would be screams of fear. There is not one Christian man in a hundred, nor in a thousand, that thinks that the whole Bible is necessary to his spiritual development and growth. Men pick and choose, and, in a sort of unconscious way, reject portions constantly. We must save them from throwing it all over. For the growth of knowledge, and of intelligence, will not permit men any longer to hold it as a talisman, an idol; and unless guided by a wiser teaching they will reject the Sacred Scriptures not only as false in science, but as a guide to conduct and to character !

We of this age have come to the mountain-top; yet we can only see the promised land of the future. Our children shall go over to the land flowing with milk and honey. Great has been the past; the future shall be yet greater. Instead of doubts and dread of ill-omened prophecies, and railings and murmurings, the Church should write upon her banner in this day of the orient, "Rise, shine; Thy light has come. The glory of the Lord is risen upon thee."

The last years of my life I dedicate to this work of religion, to this purpose of God, to this development, on a grander scale, of my Lord and Master Jesus Christ. I believe in God. I believe in immortality. I believe in Jesus Christ as the incarnated representative of the spirit of God. I believe in all the essential truths that go to make up morality and spiritual religion. I am neither an infidel, nor an agnostic, nor an atheist; but if I am anything, by the grace of God I am a lover of Jesus Christ, as the manifestation of God under the limitations of space and matter; and in no part of my life has my ministry seemed to me so solemn, so earnest, so fruitful, as this last decade will seem if I shall succeed in uncovering to the faith of this people the great truths of the two revelations—God's building revelation of the material globe, and God's building revelation in the unfolding of the human mind. May God direct me in your instruction!

III.

THE INSPIRATION OF THE BIBLE.

"Every Scripture inspired of God is also profitable for teaching, for reproof, for correction, for instruction which is in righteousness: that the man of God may be complete, furnished completely unto every good work."—II. Tim. iii : 16. (Revised Version.)

The Sacred Scriptures of the Old Testament and of the New Testament have had, and still justly have, a relation to the highest moral consciousness and to the profoundest religious experiences of the best men, and any endeavor to dethrone their influence would be met by the resistance of everything that is best in the best men.

The divine revelation, interpreted by Evolution, will in my judgment free the Sacred Scriptures from fictitious pretensions made by men, from clouds of misconceptions, and give to us the book as a clear shining light, instead of an orb veiled by false claims and worn-out philosophies. It may even be said that the Bible has been held in captivity by an untrue and unwarranted theory of inspiration which runs it against a thousand obstacles, and well-nigh leads the commentators into intellectual dishonesty. Assured, as they are, that the Bible is the word of God, upon their old theory of inspiration that word of God must be clung to, though it seemed to run against the clearest revelations of God as made plain by the researches of science. Hence, ingenuity and all forms of dishonest reasonings, for the sake of maintaining what men believed truly to be a word of God, a truth from on high;—ignoring the actual method of its growth, by laying wrong emphasis upon its external structure, and above all, making its ex-

PLYMOUTH CHURCH, Sunday morning, June 7, 1885. LESSON: Psalm cxix : 1-32.

56

terior framework—the historical mechanism—of more importance than the thing that has been secured within the Scriptures by means of that mechanism. Without the trellis surely the fruit of the vine could scarcely be much, or good; yet when the vine has, by the help of the trellis, established itself, and brought forth its fruit, the fruit and not the trellis is to be looked upon as the essential thing.

Clothes are needful to the human body; but a rent in them, though of some importance, is not a rent of the body; and even a rent in the body is not a rent of the soul that is within the body. The Bible has a value, and its history has a value, but the real value of the Bible is in the fruit of the divine Spirit which gave it authority and power, without regard to questions of authorship, of dates, of miracles, and of exterior structure.

Much that may have been needful for its evolution and production ceases to be needful for our faith in it when it has been produced. No wheat can grow without the straw, but when the straw has brought it forth, both straw and stubble perish. The wheat does not; it contains the germ of life within itself. And there are a thousand things which were employed of God's providence in the development of the truths of his word, which things are not to be held on to. They at length become the bark, and even moss on the bark, and not anything that is helpful.

1. What is the fruit which makes the Bible the tree of life to men ; and makes it, or should make it, dear to every Christian soul? What is it, looking at it in its larger light and spiritual import? Before all things the Bible is the book which has reached the highest conception of God yet attained by the human consciousness. He is *the* one and only Creator and Sustainer of the Universe which the mind ever conceived. The Universe has its unity and its harmony in him, according to the Scriptures. His being, so far as truth and disposition are concerned, can be enough understood by men to make him an object of love and obedience ; but in conditions as yet unreached by the human race God so far transcends our thought as to be unsearchable. He is our known God, and our unknown

and unsearchable God ; not in the same sense, but each in a sense separately to itself. While all pagan gods were moulded of passions, the Lord Jehovah is set forth without a stain. Rightly interpreted, even the outbursts of so-called fury and indignation on his part are not passionate, selfish, revengeful. He is righteous, and righteousness is the end sought by his government for all mankind. His indignation at all that is despicable thunders through the Word as storms in summer skies; but his lovingkindness and tender mercies surpass in expression all that is known in the literature of love among men. His long-suffering patience, his eager forgiveness, have no parallel among mankind. Whatever flaws may be picked by a narrow and carping criticism, in regard to the ideal of the Supreme Ruler of the Universe as set forth in the Scriptures, they cannot detract from the grandeur and adorableness of his character. This view pervades the Bible. Its beginning is like a rising light, but it has unfolded, and like the sun, shone brighter and brighter to the perfect day. The character of God as set forth in the Scriptures of the Old and New Testament is at once a marvel and a theme of profound gratitude; and that is one of the fruits of the Bible.

2. Next, the Bible assumes the ignorance and sinfulness of the human race. It deals with men universally as weak, helpless, needing divine guidance ; but capable of development, of rising from the animal plane to sonship with God. It practically assumes, and that from the earliest day, the true nature and condition of mankind. Evolution throws light upon the reason of this human condition, and must supplant the theories of scholastic theology on that subject. But that is the view of the Scriptures, from beginning to end,—man's helplessness, man's sinfulness, man's need of divine inspiration and regeneration. That view is unchangeable, and conforms itself entirely, and will yet more and more strikingly, to the whole theory of Evolution.

3. The Bible teaches the universal presence of God, both as the universal motive-force in matter, and as the life of human life, the light of human intelligence, the inspiration of whatever is good in human development. In him we

live and move, and have our being ; and this truth is the
mainspring. The universality and power of God's presence
are the cause of all activity, both in the material globe and in
the intellectual and moral development of the human kind.

4. The Bible gives the only grand ideal of manhood
known to literature. Great qualities have been praised by
pagans, but there has never been in any literature that I
know of anything more than dashes at the truth. From
the remotest and darkest periods, there has come to us
through the Bible the truth that Love is the organizing
center of human character, the only quality to which all
other elements of the mind will submit; the natural, organic force, which develops order and harmony. It is
more than a descant on the beauty and sweetness of personal affection. The Bible reveals Love as the Universal
Law of Humanity. Nor has this been without its commentary, in the fact that within the last two thousand years
men have been growing up into the stature and spirit of
Jesus Christ, approximately realizing this otherwise ideal
conception of what man may become.

It is not, then, a mere ideal—this book. It is a living
book, shooting out rays of light and heat into all the world.
It is clothed at this hour with the associations of myriads
of hearts who discover in it the secret of their own lives.
It is the seed-bed of all that is fine, all that is sweet, all that
is strong, all that is aspiring and ennobling in the highest human character and conduct. Every morning the sun
rolls over fields, forests, flowers, and fruits which itself has
created. The Sun of Righteousness so shines in the Bible.
It moves among men netted all over with the sweetest
and tenderest emotions of the human soul, which itself
has created as the revelation and voice of God. He who
knows only the print and the type of the book, knows only a
painted sun. What the Bible is, can be remotely appreciated
only by those who can perceive what are its fruits. Like
a cloud in summer, every drop brings forth a flower.

5. A striking quality of the Bible is its power of inspiring men with the noblest desires. The religious books of
other peoples have in them much that is good, much that

is refined in reasoning and radiant in imagination. But no other Book has had the power to change human nature, to inspire a desire to be free from sin, to develop righteousness. It is not only a Living Book, but a Book that creates life. Its track in history is like the path of the sun—filling the ages with light and growth. The very imperfections, inaccuracies, and flaws of the Bible constitute no objection to its right to be spoken of as inspired of God. The same defects occur in every other work of God. What we call polish and perfection are sure marks of mere human origin. The revelation of God in the material world is in analogy with the revelation of God in the Bible. God does not even make the best fruit without human intervention. The very imperfections of the Bible, as we consider them, are really such as might be expected in any work divinely inspired as the seed of divine life in man. They are in harmony with the other works of God. A book intended to be planted like a seed in the human mind ought not to have the finish of one intended for temporary use. Polish brings limitation. A book exactly adapted for use in New York to-day will be of no use whatever in Oregon next century. Indeed, it is very noticeable that books upon any important subject, which give the most convincing explanations and illustrations for the day of publication, ere long become almost entirely useless.

6. It is the only book that develops God in human conditions; that cheers the end of life, opening the doors of immortality; the only book, that, from beginning to end, has sympathy with the poor and weak and struggling, the sorrowful, the sinful. This is the flaming book which men fear will be destroyed; but sooner will you pluck the stars out of heaven, than one star out of this divine book! All theories of the nature of the sun may be assailed, but the sun shines on and cares naught for them. All theories respecting the history and structure of the Bible may be mooted and disputed; but there it is, a book whose fruits rise higher, smell sweeter, taste more flavorsome, inspire more health, than any or all others that have been produced upon the plane of human life.

What has the outward revelation of God's method of unfolding creation in it that can touch the inward life of the
sacred Scriptures ? What if miracles be set aside (as I do not
think they need be); what if there be anachronisms found
(as I think unquestionably there are); what if dates do conflict; what if the early notions of astronomy are proved to
be erroneous (as they are); what if six literal days of creation be no longer tenable (and they are not, except by an
unconsciously dishonest twisting of men's intellectual
faculties); what if the poem of Eden be proved but a poem,
and the legend of our first parents be shown to be but the
imagination of a childlike age: how will all the divine developments recorded in this book and proceeding from its
influence be changed by these things ? God will be the
same, and humanity will be the same. These are facts exterior to the Scriptures. The needs of man will be the same
and the supply provided will be the same. All that which
the Bible has gained and set forth to the world is untouched
by any sceptical science; and true science, the science of
real knowledge, in the hands of honest men, so far from
setting aside the word of God, step by step corroborates
that which is its interior light and its real power.

The theory of plenary and verbal inspiration is a modern
theory, which has come to its ascendancy since the Reformation. It is a theory which carries confusion into the
Bible, sets part against part, gives sanction to puerilities,
brings in contradictions, makes the early and nascent experiences of the human race of equal value with the latest
ripened truths, and subjects the Sacred Book to ridicule
and contempt. Indeed, for the most part, the infidelity of
our age springs from a theory of inspiration which has no
warrant in the Bible itself, and is contrary to the known history and structure of the Book. The logical outcome of the
theory of verbal and plenary inspiration is superstition on
the one hand, and infidelity on the other. This gigantic
folly sprang from the apparent necessity of Protestant theologians after breaking with Rome. The Catholic made the
Church infallible. Against that claim it became necessary
to set up the Bible as the only infallible authority; and

every thought, every record, every fact, every custom, was believed to have been enunciated to the writers, who were regarded as reporters, amanuenses, or mere clerks, appointed to put down God's thoughts.

There can be no question that the disclosures of geology respecting the six days of creation have controverted the popular apprehension in regard to the accounts of creation in the earlier chapters of Genesis.

It may be said that, generally speaking, the scientific world has set aside ruthlessly and without a moment's hesitation the whole of this history of the creation. There are moral results from the declaration in Genesis of the unity of God as the one and sole Creator of the whole world, that will be preserved; and although there are a great many Christian geologists—like Professor Guyot, late of Princeton College, and like Professor Dana, now of Yale, New Haven—who have undertaken to harmonize statements of the early chapters in Genesis with the facts that geology has laid bare and made certain, yet even Professor Dana takes the ground that if we are to refuse the help of science in exegetical interpretation—if we stand on the ground of exegesis alone—everything is gone, and the revelation of science will end the delusion of the six literal days of creation.

The ingenuity, not to say the unconscious intellectual dishonesty, of men in their endeavor to reconcile facts with fiction would cease if this false and vicious theory of verbal and plenary inspiration were abandoned.

That the human mind may be stimulated by God to a higher exercise of its own powers, is not to be doubted. That this was the way in which many holy men of old were led to speak, need not be doubted. But the literal and verbal theory makes mere channels of the sacred writers, and rolls through them the thoughts and statements of God. It makes God the historian, and suspends the natural functions of the human mind. The human intellect is thus made, like a trumpet, an instrument to be spoken through.

There is another theory of inspiration, which not only

saves the Book by reconciling it with the other and indubitable revelation of God in nature, but which frees it
from a thousand criticisms and objections; and is sufficient to maintain the integrity of the Book. It assumes
that God is the life universal; that whatever is force
or energy directly or remotely proceeds from the nature of
God's own being. How God infuses himself into mind or
matter no one knows. It is somewhat a parallel, although
by a small measure of comparison, with that which every
man is conscious of in his own experience. We know that
we are creatures of intelligence and volition, and we know
that our intelligence and volition, and all that which makes
the upper man in ourselves, coheres in and is, in some way
or other, within the organization of the human body. But
can anybody tell what the principle of vitality is ? Nobody
can; nobody does. Can anybody tell what the connection
is between the mind-operation and the brain, or any of the
organs of the whole human body ? We know that we have
a physical body subject to great physical laws; and we know
that, pervading it somehow, somewhere, there is also something that is not matter, and that is the most effectual and
characteristic element in us. That which we recognize in
ourselves has only to be enlarged to become an analogy of
that which is grander ; and to give us some vague idea of
the connection that subsists between the developed universe and the ever-presence of the divine Intelligence and
the divine Will.

This is not Pantheism, which makes the universe, in its
totality, God. As a poetic dream I could conceive of Pantheism having a toleration; but as seeking an explanation
of difficulties I cannot conceive how a man should hold a
sober face and enunciate it, because the thing that is an
explanation is more unexplained and inexplicably mysterious, and utterly dark to the understanding, than the dif-
ficulty which it undertakes to make clear. That there are
difficulties in the relation between God and humanity, and
between God and the world, nobody doubts. That must
be, from the nature and the pre-eminent largeness of God
himself. God is not matter; God is not in matter. That

is, we have no reason to say so.   Yet all laws, all susceptibilities, issue from him.   They are the result of his intelligence and of his will.   Their power is the continuous power
of God as the life of the world.   The universe is a perpetual
outgoing from the mind of God; and yet God is separable
from this material universe in his existence and methods.

Now, the Bible is inspired of God, I have said.   We are
to bear in mind that his inspiration—the in-breathing of
his power, of his thought, of his will—is the cause of everything in the universe.   The Bible, as I look upon it, is
the record in part of what the influence of God's Spirit
moving on human consciousness has brought to pass along
the course of one national history.   It is the record in a
particular line of the effect of that universal and continuous action of the divine mind on the human mind, that has
raised man from the lowest barbaric depths, step by step,
unfolding moralities, social life, all graces, all affections, all
reason, all the treasures of moral nature, and all spirituali-
ties.   It is *the human race* that has been inspired; and the
Bible in every part of it was *lived*, first, and the record of it
made afterwards.   As a great poet never originates, but only
throws into masterful forms the sum of all the thoughts
and feelings that exist down to his time; as Shakespeare
did not create his characters, but saw them, and with
genius had the power to gather them together in groups
and unfold them, not as anything that was new, but as that
which was existing, though incoherent, dispersed, inorganic; so, the race itself was inspired to growth, and
lived until some results of experience had become wide-
spread and vaguely recognized.   The time came when
a man of large nature, feeling more sensitively the impulse of the divine inspiration, was able to gather, to
fix, and give out as a truth these unorganized elements
—never perhaps before put into regular form and spoken.
They were found out to be real and authoritative before
he declared it.   Many good things in civil laws are,
comparatively speaking, laws by public sentiment before
they become authoritative laws by legislative enact-
ment.   So there are myriads of truths that are unfolded in

action and in fact long before authority is given them by anybody that declares them, crying "Thus saith the Lord!" God does say so; but he says so first through the findings-out, through the trials, the failures and mistakes, the successes and ascertainments, of actual human experience. And so the Word of God is the record along one line of a grand experiment, namely, the high development of men from the lowest point of possible human existence through the experiences of human life.

Men found out, step by step, in primitive days, the difference between right and wrong, selfishness and helpfulness, justice and injustice, cruelty and kindness, the truth and falsehoods, purity and lust. Men slowly learned to labor, to labor conjointly; to look forward and store their harvests, and so came foresight, frugality, and the self-denial required in sacrificing the pleasure of to-day for the sake of yet greater good in the future. While it is to be believed that the divine Spirit at special times and seasons rouses the faculties of men, develops them to their highest power, yet, in regard to the grand elements of life, its laws, its civilization, political economy, sociology, governments, men have been led along the slow steps of evolution.

If this be the subject-nature of the inspiration of the Bible, see how it works. The things that have been found out and accepted by mankind—the great spiritual experiences of love that are recorded in the Bible—whether chanted by David or glowing in the eloquence of Paul, or lying, sweet as unuttered music, in the breast of John—all the elements that belong to the highest human nature have been steadily unfolded in fact and reality by the course of providence through long periods of time; and, having come into existence, under divine inspiration, they have taken their declared form in the word of God; and they are never, never to be stricken out.

But, on the other hand, there are a great many things in the Bible that were believed in in an earlier day, and are not true. Take the early accounts given in Genesis; they were legends before they were history. They were grouped together. They were the earliest conceptions that the

5

human race had, as it started on its tentative journey towards final spiritual civilization. These were the earliest thoughts; and they are as precious to us as to a mother are the earliest utterances of her babe, who remembers them, writes them down, recalls them, ponders them, talks of them. Yet when compared with the later-developed wisdom in the child they are as nothing. It is a great thing to know what were the thoughts of men at their earliest stages, and at the next step, and the next. This was the way in which the world at that time thought that creation had come into being,—in six literal days of twenty-four hours. There are two wrong-headed classes of men now. There are the ignorant and obstinate that still believe in this ; there are the scientific, sceptical men who do not believe a word in it, and who, therefore, throw away the Bible as being a book of falsehoods, that cannot be inspired. But a book that undertakes to register the imperfect stages through which men passed may be an inspired book after all, and the book of God. Thus monogamy was tried, and found to be the true social condition; but polygamy existed, was recognized as a fact and legislated for, according to the early Scriptures, and so, if the Bible is the word of God according to the old theory of plenary direct inspiration, Mormonism is right; and that is its stronghold to-day. The Mormons believe in the Old Testament—they believe in it earnestly and literally. If any man should hold to absolute inspiration, according to the old verbal theory, how shall he get away from the facts of the Old Testament? Mormonism cannot be wrong if God inspired it, and taught it in his book.

There was a period of time when it was a great thing for a man's life to be saved, and it was held better that he should be a slave than be slaughtered. But, little by little, men found out that slavery was an inconvenience. True, in the Hebrew time, first of all the Oriental nations, it was made impracticable, not by directly forbidding it but by making it so burdensome that they could not afford to keep it up, and so let it die out. Yet, that it is recognized as existing, without rebuke, in the Old Testament and the New, is uncontradictable. In the great controversy that preceded our greater settlement by the sword, this was the argument of the pro-slavery pulpits of the North and the pulpits of the South, namely, that slavery cannot be wrong because it existed in the times of Christ, and was not forbidden of him or of his apostles; it was practiced under the Old Testament dispensation, and laws were made for it, and thus it was recognized and regulated by God,—"the patriarchal institution," it was called.

It might as well be said that because early men had wooden plows God approved wooden plows instead of iron ones. When the iron was changed into steel and the whole structure of the plow was made conformable to easy passage, what then? Did God not approve it because it is not mentioned in the Bible? The very theory of creation is that God set men with appropriate faculties upon the plane of life, and sent them forward by universal influences beating in upon them, by all necessities, by all laws, and let them find their own way on and up. So every flower had to come up, so every bird, so every beast, everywhere ; and so men came up. Was there then no guiding divine Providence? But is not that a Providence which makes use of natural laws? Is there any evidence that God ever works except through law? Is not the direct action of God's mind upon the human mind, giving to it unwonted force and sensibility, an act under law?

All the thoughts and laws and ideas and institutions of men came from God, not directly, as the light falls on vegetation, but mediately, through the influences of life, through the pressure of institutions, through the power of laws unconscious to men upon whom they were acting. The record of this book says precisely that. Now, when men say, "Slavery is right because it is in the Old Testament," I say, What is it in the Old Testament for? Simply because it was one of those early experiments that in the end destroyed itself. We have the record of it, not the authorization; just the record.

Things that are very natural in a child would be very unnatural in a grown-up man. A record of the infancy of the

world must contain a multitude of things then permitted
but since outgrown. Shall one play at sixty the games
which suited him at six? Has not the world grown? Have
not human thoughts grown? Is there not clearer light?

Thus we find in the word of God there is an ascending
development. The earliest periods are very simple. Men's
thought of God was very simple and uncomplex. It grew
more and more complex and loftier. The portraiture of
man in the earlier periods recorded in the Scriptures is
very dim, almost undiscernible in many relations; but the
thought of what man is, and what his duty is, and what his
possibilities are, steadily ascends all the way through until
we come to later ages. Then we begin to hear higher utterances; then human nature has ascended to that condition
in which it is possible for the mind to live in the personal
atmosphere of God; and as God acts through physical law
upon matter, so he acts through mental and spiritual law
upon the conscious faculties of human nature, giving them
power to discern, to collect, to authenticate, and to an-
nounce great truths.

The difference, then, is between this theory of natural
growth and the old popular notion—what may be called
the scholastic, theological notion—as if God had said to a
man, "Sit down and write what I am going to tell you."
That is the general and clouded notion of most men now.

But, to recapitulate, we hold the Bible to be the record of
the gradual and progressive unfolding of human knowledge in respect to social and spiritual things through vast
periods of time; and the inspiration of God consisted in
the impulse by natural law, by social institutions, by reflection, by experiment, by the findings-out of human life little
by little, and finally by that direct and personal influence
of the divine nature which did arouse and stimulate the
human faculties to their highest sensibility and activity,
under the conditions existing. Then comes the recording
of truths and deeds by men competent to understand, and
to give out the largest idea of them, whether in devotional
form, or in song and psalm, or in philosophical, moral, and
spiritual declarations. The "holy men of old" were men

above their day, that were able to concentrate in their own
consciousness the meaning of all those things that had been
gradually found out by myriads of men, and give them an
authentic and, in general, with increasing frequency, a
glorious form in the word of God.

The Bible, then, is the record of the results of Divine inspiration on mankind, principally in one line of national
history. It is the history of the unfolding of the social,
moral, and spiritual sense of the human race. Holy men
of old were moved by a divine impulse to give expression;
to give authorized force and form; not to discover, not to
invent, but to give authoritative form and special application to that which had already been ascertained as the fruit
of experience.

I am aware that many persons, especially if they have not
given much thought to the matter, are not much troubled
with the old view; and no man need be troubled with it
if he will not read the Bible, or if he reads it and does
not reflect. But with men who are hungering for knowledge, and are obliged to compare things with things, and
to think, there has been, and there is yet, a very great diffi-
culty that prevents the Bible from working its best effects
upon them by reason of what seems to be error or incon-
sistency. But if the Bible records the progress of ideas,
there must be infantine ideas in it. These are not God's
legislation. They are the record of how men came in
thought and feeling up to a given time, and they are historic
steps tracing the development—in other words, the evolution—of great moral truths in human consciousness.

But, it will be said, "How can men be certain, then, of
the truth? What we want is an infallible standard. What
we want is a book which we know to be the direct expression of the mind and will of God." Well, have you such
a Bible on the old theory? Large classes of educated,
thoughtful, and disciplined men, down to this day, have
held this doctrine of direct plenary inspiration of the Scriptures. They have, in other words, held the book to be an
absolute and infallible standard of truth ; and the result is
that there are about as many different understandings of

the book as there have been different schools through all time. So far from having unity and certainty, the Christian Church has been in a state of distraction and revolution, in a state of quarrelling and persecution, all the world over and in all time. There is scarcely a square league that has not a separate sect in it, and all of them cry, "Thus saith the Lord!" In the Bible itself they find reason to differ and to quarrel with each other, and have a hundred different interpretations of the book which, men say, would end all controversy. It did not end all controversy; it never has ended controversy; it never will end controversy. You must find some larger formula than that. No man can be in union with his fellow-man absolutely through the medium of the understanding, for the understanding itself is not alike and of the same constant and absolute quality in all men. The understanding sometimes means intellect and poetry, sometimes intellect and imagination, sometimes intellect and love, sometimes intellect and hate, sometimes intellect and any or all of the passions, or all of the moral qualities in a man's nature. What men see, they see through the color of the feeling that infuses itself into their thinking faculty. You cannot bring men into unity in this way. If there were a hundred men with a hundred different gauges of eye, one sees things only at the minutest point, and the next man a shade larger, and the next man two shades larger, and the other men clear up to the hundred, by constant increments. If they should undertake to say how long and large a thing was, and every man should judge by his own eye, there would be a hundred sects in that hundred men, and they would all be quarrelling together because that which sees is different in them. There are certain mathematical truths about which men cannot disagree; they are absolute: but in regard to all moral truths and social truths where the feelings must of necessity come in, it is utterly impossible that men should absolutely agree.

The two revelations of matter and of mind are, in regard to structure, strikingly alike. This is the foundation of Bishop Butler's famous treatise on the doctrine of natural and revealed religion. God's revelation in matter has in it a certain striking resemblance to his revelation in mind. The revelation of God in matter left to be interpreted by experience and experiment, has laid the foundations of science, and has attained to a degree and scope of relative certainty such as has never been gained in any other field. Now, the truths evolved by society are just as stable. You say you cannot tell what is right and what is wrong, unless there is an absolute command of God for it, and unless it stands on the authority of God's declaration. But you can. God says, "Thou shalt not steal." You do not believe that stealing is bad because God said so; you believe it from what you know of the thing itself. "Thou shalt not murder." You do not believe it simply because God spake it. God gave his lawgiver of old inspiration to declare that which men had already found out of this social truth. And you believe that murder is wrong, because of the nature of murder, not on account of the source from which the declaration came. There are thousands of things that men believed in early days because some authority told them, but in later days, because they have risen to a higher standpoint and know them in and of themselves. It may be said that the civilized pagan world (if we may so speak) and the Christian world are much nearer together in regard to the great truths on which men in this life stand, than they believe themselves to be. The things that we have found out from the human race by the experiment of living are the grand foundation of moral truths, and about these the sects do not disagree. To love God, to love our fellow-men, to be faithful to obligations, to hold in honor all duties of fidelity, honesty, truth, purity, courage, self-denial, industry, frugality, regard for justice and for society—there is not a man who doubts the beauty and the authentic worth of these things.

In what realm are the differences, then, among Christian men, between sect and sect? They are in regard to those things that transcend human experience, of which we have reasonable faith, but which we never can subject to our own investigation;—the nature of Divine being, whether

God is one or threefold; the nature of God's decrees, the question of his fore-ordination or his foresight; the question of man's final salvation or reprobation; all these things that transcend any experiment or any possible human investigation, and which men take on what they say to be the testimony of the Scriptures—these they quarrel over. The structure of a church; we have not a shred of testimony about it except in the Old Testament, and that has all gone under. Does not all the Christian world bombard all the Jewish world, and that which is sacred to the Jew is rejected almost as a token of unorthodoxy by the Christian world to-day. The old institutions have lapsed in order to give birth to newer and better ones. The things on which men quarrel are those that are supposed to proceed from some divine authority, which, however, they never are able to agree in interpreting—the proper power of the priesthood, the method of organizing the church, the divine nature of government (except so far as it has been expressed in the findings-out of human experiment and human consciousness),—the Christian world has been split into a hundred different warring sects on these questions.

It is said, "If you take this dangerous view of the interpretation of the Scriptures every man will aspire to become a master, and will presume to take just what he chooses out of the Bible." Yes, that is so. That is just the way we have been doing about nature, and what we are doing to this day about all knowledge. God made the world just as it is. He never set up a sign, "This is a rock; do not let it fall on you." Man learned that. God never said, "Moss and grass are different." Man found it out. He never said anything with regard to lightning striking a man; man found out that for himself, a little later. In regard to everything that we have actual knowledge of, we have come to that knowledge by the slow process of finding out. Human life has crept up the inclined plane, not inch by inch, but by the millionth of an inch, at a time. So too men will find and take from the Bible that which they need —and each for himself. We do it on any theory. Men put together five or six hundred unrelated texts out of the Bible, and others stand over against them with as many more on the other side. Their "divine word" speaks with no certain voice. But on taking away the untenable theory of verbal and plenary inspiration, you remove all those sources of offence. Give up the attempt to indorse upon God's government things which we know to have sprung from the weakness of humanity, though the record of them is made in his Bible, and you take away the very weapons of infidelity; and, on the other hand, the moment that you accept the spiritual results of all time, recorded in "Sacred Scripture," the "fruits of the Spirit"—love, joy, peace, longsuffering, gentleness, goodness, self-control—the moment that you clasp hands together upon these indubitable unfoldings of the spirit and of the evolution of man's moral nature, which are recorded in the Bible, that very moment there cannot be infidelity. Nobody wants to deny those things. There is not a man that lives on the face of the earth who does not know that love is beautiful, and desire it in his friends, and in himself, and toward himself. There is not a man who does not believe that peace in this turbulent and thundering world is the one thing that seems almost an impossible luxury, and yet every man craves it. Love, joy; O, what hunger for joy! O, what fantastic contrivances to obtain it; joy which shall fill a man full! The whole world wants joy. Bring forth, then, the religion which shall have for its characteristic elements love, joy, peace, longsuffering, gentleness, goodness. Does any one wish with miscreant club to brain *that* Bible? Yet that combination of noble characteristics is the very meaning of the sacred Scriptures! Who wants to destroy it? What sect could rise up against the real meaning of the Bible?

What then is left? What has the Bible to offer us, as the "Word of God"? What law of growth does it give us, that we can depend upon? Let me answer this by reading a passage from the Second Epistle of Peter:

"Grace and peace be multiplied unto you through the knowledge of God, and of Jesus our Lord, according as his divine power hath given unto us all things that pertain unto life and godliness, through the knowl-edge of him that hath called us to glory and virtue: whereby are given unto us exceeding great and precious promises: that by these ye might be partakers of the divine nature, having escaped the corruption that is in the world through lust.

"And besides this, giving all diligence, add to your faith virtue; and to virtue, knowledge; and to knowledge, temperance; and to temperance, patience; and to patience, godliness; and to godliness, brotherly kind-ness; and to brotherly kindness, charity.

"For if these things be in you, and abound, they make you that ye shall neither be barren nor unfruitful in the knowledge of our Lord Jesus Christ. Wherefore the rather, brethren, give diligence to make your calling and election sure: for if ye do these things, ye shall never fall: for so an entrance shall be ministered unto you abundantly into the ever-lasting kingdom of our Lord and Saviour Jesus Christ."

IV.

THE SINFULNESS OF MAN.

"For the earnest expectation of the creature waiteth for the manifestation of the sons of God. For the creature was made subject to vanity, not willingly, but by reason of him who hath subjected the same in hope; because the creature itself also shall be delivered from the bondage of corruption into the glorious liberty of the children of God. For we know that the whole creation groaneth and travaileth in pain together until now."—Romans viii: 19-22.

I believe that it is out of the power of any man to give a connected and perfect interpretation of these two immortal chapters, the Seventh and the Eighth of Romans, except upon the substantial theory of Evolution; and when in the light of this more recent discovery the method of God in creation, both of the terraqueous globe and of animal and human life, shall have been explored and perfectly understood, both of these chapters will come out into a prominence that they have never had, though they have fascinated the attention of all Christian scholars.

If we consider man as a dual creature,—subordinately an animal, with a superinduced spiritual being, an animal at the bottom and a spiritual being at the top, and the two struggling together for supremacy,—the seventh chapter of Romans will be very thoroughly interpreted as a commentary on the facts set forth by science and history. If we enter into the eighth chapter of Romans with the understanding that men have advanced to a period in which the direction of the soul of God upon their souls has given them a victory over their animal nature, we shall begin to

SUNDAY MORNING, June 14, 1885. LESSON : John xiv; Romans viii.

75

sound the depths of this wonderful chapter. And we shall
see flashes of philosophy, strange to any Hebrew mind,—
strange in Paul's,—yet manifest here, revealing in some
sort, an account of why the world has been made as it has
been.

In that passage which I have selected for the gate
through which to pass to my subject to-day, we have this
simple declaration, that the whole of creation has been in
a turmoil and trouble; that it was not man's fault that he
was born "subject to vanity,"—that is, to changeableness,
—to that change which carries him from stage to stage.
It was a part of God's plan. The creature was made subject to diversity and change, not voluntarily, of his own
will, but "by reason of him who hath subjected the same in
hope;" by reason of God, whose long foresight saw what was
to take place, because the creature,—that is, man, the human
creature,—shall be "delivered from the bondage of corruption."   Born an animal, he shall be delivered from animalism into the glorious liberty of the children of God; beginning at the bottom of the scale, he shall terminate at the
top; beginning environed by matter and largely subject to
its inevitable laws, with instincts and appetites that ally him
downwards, as well as tendencies that prophesy an upward
career, he shall pass through all these transitions, and in the
end the human race shall be evolved into a glorious liberty.
The beginnings are struggle and bondage; the issue is a
sweeping and final victory.

It must not be supposed that, because the divine method
of creation has been substantially discovered—because in
the thought of the scientific world it has passed a period of
doubt and controversy, and has become the working theory
of scientific minds—therefore all difficulties belonging to it
have been solved.   It must not be thought that all applications of it to nature, to society, and to religious questions
are already settled.   There is yet much *terra incognita;* there
are many spheres of uncertainty.   The world has almost
infinite contents, and we know comparatively but a portion
of them.   The art of Discovery has been so developed that
new material is coming up every day for consideration, and

the relation of discoveries to old truths must be modified. The theory of Evolution may be said to be in the condition of an incomplete railway; the line has been determined on and explored, the grubbing and grading are quite advanced, and indeed parts of the road are completed and in use; but there is yet many a cut and fill, many a bridge, many a league without superstructure; long tracts unfit as yet for commerce. But its career is not doubtful. In its rude and yet unuseable conditions it is the prophet of its own perfect state.

For a long time speculative theology ruled man's beliefs. Character and conduct, which are the great ends of God in the creation of man, were supposed to be the product chiefly of right systematic and scholastic beliefs. It is not to be denied that right beliefs have much to do with conduct and with character, but it is false to suppose that conduct and character can always and easily be derived from systematic theological beliefs. A system grew up which has been filled with confusion and has had the effect of confusing mankind; and it has come to pass that theology stands in about this state : those who think they understand it dispute incessantly among themselves, and those who do not wish to quarrel do not try to understand it. Systematic theology includes in a general way, to be sure, a sound morality, an imperfect mental philosophy, an analysis of God's nature and government, in which good and evil, truth and fiction, are blended, as in Daniel's vision; and this vision is an admirable description of the present condition of theology. The image's head was of fine gold, his breast and arms were of silver, his belly and thighs of brass, his legs of iron, his feet part iron and part clay. So stands theology to-day.

In the popular mind this scheme of organized and systematic belief is confounded with religion. But it is not religion; it is not the cause of religion: it is often only in juxtaposition. Theology is confounded with Christianity; and because certain elements of theology have been exploded, men say, "Where is your Christianity? Much of it has gone already, and the rest will follow." The greatest

part of current theological lore was neither taught or even
alluded to by Jesus, the Christ; and yet men are eager to
say that when theology is disrupted to be recomposed,
Christianity is also disrupted and to be reconstructed.   The
two things are wide apart.   The regnant systems of theology are inferential, artificial; philosophically, they are
either imperfect or false.   It is this system which foresees
the danger to itself from Evolution, and that cries out
against the new light.

Now let us inquire whether the theory of Evolution, the
method of God in the creation of the world, is likely to
affect favorably or unfavorably the fundamental elements
of Christianity, as it was taught by Christ himself.

Consider, first, the universality of the Divine presence as
the force acting upon mankind and upon nature.   The
doctrine of the presence of God everywhere, in all, as the
one great force that is working in nature and in human
life, is nowhere so significantly taught as by Jesus, and
recorded by John.   He is not a God that has invented the
world and stands like an engineer to see how it runs; not a
God afar off, a mechanical God; not an architectural God,
a builder that does not live in his own building; but a God
universally diffused, to such an extent that wherever there
is force, there is God behind that force.   Certainly this
doctrine of the universality of the Divine presence will not
be upset, but substantiated.   Though Agnostic and Atheistic reasoners should rename God, and call him "Force"
or "Energy," I care not; if by that they mean, as they
must, what we mean by "Jehovah," by "Lord," by "God,"
they can make a name to suit themselves.   The name is
not the thing, but the qualities that are under it; and if
there be one thing that is to be triumphantly demonstrated
by Evolution, it is that the whole life of the world is per-
meated by the life of God himself.

Then, the doctrine of the universal sinfulness and imperfection of human nature: is man born sinless, blameless,
and is that his character as revealed in history?   Is that
his character now?   Is the doctrine of human sinfulness—
not the awkward phrase "total depravity," a spawn of an

illegitimate philosophy—a phrase misleading and inappropriate—but the doctrine that man, and every man always and everywhere, is a sinful creature, is that likely to be substantiated or to be overthrown by Evolution? The absolute necessity of a change in mankind from the control of the flesh to the supreme control of the moral sentiments, or, if we want the old phrases, "conversion," "regeneration," the being "born again"—is that truth likely to be obliterated, or enforced and fortified?

The human mind is far from being explored—especially in the reach of its faculties, and in their possible developments. This is true not only of the intellectual faculties, but of the emotions and moral sentiments. The average development of the mass of mankind is very low. Single men shoot up above their fellows with phenomenal powers. Men of genius, seers, prophets, seem hardly allied to the inferior multitude. Has the end been reached? Are there to be developed no higher capabilities? Is it not possible that a degree of sensibility may be attained that shall make the soul susceptible to the pressure and direct inspiration of the Divine Being? The steps of this analogy are seen in the inferior animal kingdom. They rise in susceptibility and power as they ascend in organization. In the humankind, the lower tier have but glimpses of those experiences which have become common to the higher. Barbarism and civilization designate the human mind undeveloped and highly developed. Does not Evolution point towards this explicit teaching of Jesus regarding the unity of man with God?

Nay more: the control of mind over matter is taught in Christianity; that is, when men, drawn up by the Spirit of God, have come so far into his presence as to be filled with his vitality, in a limited degree, they have given to them something of divine power. Many of the mysterious and utterly unregulated exhibitions which we are seeing now, which are without form and void, like the earth itself at creation's dawn, seem to be in that border-land of which Christ himself teaches us, asserting that it is in the power of men by fasting and prayer to rise to such a height that they can control not only demoniac spirits, but **exter-nal** matter itself. That my spirit can control as much matter as I have in my body, we do not doubt ; but the control over matter exterior to one's self and not organized into one's self,—is that a hard thing to compass? Christ says that it can be done. It can be done by those that rise, expanding in themselves to such a state that they are like God, and receive as it were a divine impulse and with it divine power.

But there is something further: there is also taught in Christianity the truth that its sincere votaries not only receive divine influence, but are enabled to reciprocate in some faint degree, and to act upon the Divine nature ; as a little child has power over its parent, not by its hand nor by its foot, nor by its whole body, but by playing with its little affections upon the affections of its superior and parent—"a little child shall lead them." So it has been from the beginning, and so it will be to the end, on that same principle—the pure in heart shall see God ; and when men come to that stage in which right things desired can be obtained by the impulse, the imploration of the soul upon God, he is affected. Though he works through laws and a continuity of laws, yet there is a large commonwealth of liberties by which a man can produce effects through God, that cannot be produced in any other way.

Here is one answer to the skeptical doubts about prayer. Christ broke up the provincial and degenerate notions of the contemporary Jews; for the Jews of his day are not to be confounded with the reverent and authoritative and in-spired Jews of the elder day. There had been a backslid-ing and a degradation in the Jews among whom Jesus lived, and he broke up their small and narrow notions that God was by covenant their national god, as distinguished from any and all other nations; likewise the low notion of faith held by the Greek philosophers, and the mechanical Ro-man notions of divine government as a vast machine of invincible laws which God would not change, and man could not. Jesus taught in distinction from these that there were buried in mankind the elements of a liberty like God's own, and that if minds and lives were unfolded to the extent possible, they should be redeemed from the hard conditions of inferior laws, from the mechanical inevitableness of material force, from matter, and come into the glorious liberty of the sons of God. Christ also brought to light life and immortality; he painted these coming evolutions in the soul of man upon the background of a radiant immortality.

Now, the sum of all this is that man is, at a primary observation, an animal, a low-toned, ignorant, sinful being ; that it was not necessary that he should remain so; that there was a power in him of unfolding by which he should steadily gain advantage and ascendency over his lower and animal nature; that when the rays of the divine soul touched his and translated him to a higher sphere, he should then come into direct and personal conscious communion with God; and that when the predominant moral sensibilities were stimulated and brought to their superior stages of growth by the intouch of God's nature, they should not only have the power of outsight, foresight, and insight—intuition—but that they should have such a communion with God as that they should be conscious of his presence all the time; and in this intimate communion of the soul with its Creator in this higher range man should have something of divine power, and might be called really set free from all animalism, and mainly from the subverting influences of his fleshly conditions.

That is the teaching of Christianity; is it not also that of Evolution ? Is not that the most glorious application that has ever been made of the fact of an ascending scale by which men, beginning at organized matter and steadily going up from animal to the social, to the moral, to the intellectual, and to the spiritual, at last find out their birthplace, their birthright, and by a successive series of unfoldings learn that God is their God and that they are his children ? This is the doctrine of the evolution of forces in life; of the unfolding of all that lies in the seed, of all that lies in matter, by steady development of natural laws; of all that lies in human society by the gradual stages of civilization; of all

6

that belongs to morality by its steady unfolding and advance; of all that belongs to spirituality, and last and most glorious, the unfolding of the whole man so that he becomes "partaker of the divine nature."

Let us take up one point this morning, namely: the question of Man's Sinfulness.

The doctrine of universal sinfulness has been a theme of very great dispute among theologians. I was born into the power of thinking just in the midst of that controversy that was going on in Boston and throughout New England between the Unitarian and Orthodox clergy: the Orthodox declaring that men were totally depraved; and the Unitarian of Dr. Channing's school declaring that they were not, that there was very much good in them, and that what they needed was not a total reconstruction, but simply a change of emphasis, and that education or unfolding would bring the man up step by step to very high conditions, that he was a virtuous creature when he had been gradually unfolded and educated, and that it was not fair to call the pure, unsuspicious, loving, upright maiden, with all resplendent virtues, "totally depraved." Well, the Unitarians were right; and the Orthodox were right—except in terminology. They were not right in their philosophy, they were not right in supposing that the fall of Adam had so corrupted the very body and soul of man that he could not, until he was absolutely changed by the grace of God, do a single thing that was agreeable to God. They mistook the road: they were right as to the fact of man's universal sinfulness; they were wrong as to the cause of it and of the nature of it.

The capacity, the duty of unfolding from the animal to the spiritual state, has been held almost without contradiction. And the doctrine of the universal presence of God in which was that stimulating power needed by man to unfold him from the animal to the spiritual, laid a foundation for prayer, for the belief in a personal superintending Providence, for such a control of inferior laws as shall produce what are loosely called miracles, which in their nature are but the ascendency of mind over matter. This doctrine of the universality of the divine presence and of the power given to the human will and reason by participation in it, laid the foundation for beliefs in personal providence in particular, for prayer, for communion with God, and for the attainment of power of working by natural laws something higher than one can get by ordinary force of law.

Now, what is there in the doctrine of Evolution that contradicts these sublime disclosures of man's nature and his relations to God? Is not the whole tendency of facts, as reflected by the new light on God's method of creation, in favor of this noble theology? Man was born at the bottom on purpose. It was the creative and organic decree that he should begin at the bottom and work his way up steadily until he reached the very top, until, as it were, his life was mingled with the divine life.

Sin is technically called in the Scriptures "the transgression of the law." All sin is transgression of the law; but all transgression of the law is not sin. A man may break ten thousand laws and not sin once. Your little child breaks laws before he knows how to keep his finger out of the fire; before he knows anything about the doctrine of gravitation he tumbles out of bed or down-stairs; and before he knows anything about what is wholesome or unwholesome he crowds into his mouth whatever he can lay his hands on. You do not punish him, or consider him punishable. He violates whole bundles of laws every day; and in every household we know perfectly well that while wrong consists in violation of just commands, yet all violation of just commands is not blameworthy. There are other elements to come in. By creation man began at the bottom, whatever theory of origin may be adopted. If you say that he is a being that in the regular order and analogy of nature is ascendant from the lower stages of creation, I incline to that view as a hypothesis; not as a thing proved, nor in any absolute sense exactly provable, but as a thing carrying many probabilities and throwing much light upon many questions of human life. But whatever may be our theory, whether it is that men developed out of the lower animal life, or were started at the bottom by a special creation of

the human race, one or the other of these is to be held by
every one, and both of them lead to the like results.   Man
is, and always has been, an unfolding creature, beginning
at simple and going towards the complex, beginning at
the little and gathering and gaining more and more.   In
this evolution of the human family each step higher leaves
it inferior to the station above.

In sin lies the conflict between the lower elements in
human nature and the higher,—between the flesh and the
spirit.   An animal cannot sin.   That is right in him which
would be wrong in man.   Appetites and passions, without
reason or conscience, cannot sin.   When social and moral
susceptibilities are developed, duty is developed, and conflict between the animal and spiritual elements; and sin is
the insubordination of the inferior parts to the law of the
superior.   St. Paul's reasoning in the seventh of Romans is
conclusive to the effect that sin is the persistence of animal
passions against the control of the moral sentiments.

Imperfection is the indispensable concomitant of gradual
development.   If the ideal condition of man be assumed
as the measurement, there is no perfect man, nor has
there ever been a perfect man.   That is, if you take that
to which God designs man to come, and measure him in
any stage of his development, at that stage he is imperfect
as compared with the ideal.   All men either have dwelt
in their lower nature contentedly, playing the part of intelligent animals, or have quickened morally,—they have
struggled upward, and there has been a steady conflict
between their lower selves and their higher.   They have
still to struggle in a condition of imperfection—imperfection of knowledge, of will, of power of obedience to the
supreme law of duty.   They have been steadily unfolding,
and this unfolding process carries with it a double effect,
namely, superiority to inferior conditions gained, and in-
feriority to the conditions that yet are to be gained with
limited responsibility.

Sinfulness is universal, and inevitable to undeveloped
manhood.   Sin is the voluntary violation of known law.
But to a large extent theology has included "infirmity"

with sin. Both are transgressions of the law; but all viola-
tions of law are not sinful. Sin is of the will; infirmity is
of ignorance and weakness. Men have not learned how to
use the faculties which in ascending gradations demand
vast experience. It is the richness of human nature that
confuses man and makes duty so difficult. Shall the hand
require long practice before it works skillfully and achieves
success, and the mind not demand time, culture, practice,
before it can work harmoniously within itself, and amid
the external distractions of social and civil life? Men are
responsible for sin, but not for infirmity. Infirmities are
the mistakes which men make on their way to knowledge.
Life is a trade, to be learned; a profession, to be gained by
education; an art, requiring long drill. Man must learn his
trade: the most complex, the most subtle, and the most
difficult that ever was learned. No man learns it except by
help of institutions, by public sentiment, by direct moral
influences, brought to bear upon him. The education of a
man should unfold his nature in harmony with himself, in
harmony with his fellows, in harmony with God. The
knowledge of how a man shall ascend from the control of
his animal instincts requires a training, an education, that
is not learned in a day, and was learned by the race only
through slow-creeping centuries.

Suppose you attempt to carry on a household as theologists try to carry on churches. You would extinguish it.
You are obliged first to treat your child as an animal. Of
course poetry has always called children "angels," but
those who bring them up do not. You know very well that
a child has to be treated as a little untaught, mischievous
animal. The more largely endowed and stronger the child
is in knowledge and will, the more reprobate the little animal may be in the beginning. You have to treat the child
at the start on the medical plan of counter-irritation, and
you correct, not by reason, but by the palm of your hand,
by a counter-irritation that stops the selfishness, or the disobedience. You know that it is a slow and gradual process
by which at last the child begins to have a sense of the
rights of others. It has a distinct period of unfolding,

when it comes to learn the elements of social morality.
These are learned in the narrow family circle first. When
he is still further advanced, he is taught to feel that morality extends its sphere and includes communities, and that
he belongs to his race, and that every man is his neighbor
who has need of his services and sympathies. That is a
later stage of perfection. The last of all is spirituality, and
spirituality with regard to multitudes of men has too short
a summer, and the frost cuts off the bud before it comes to
blossom. It is the latest stage, the most difficult, and the
resultant of all the others, but a real and possible stage.

No ; you cannot afford to treat your children on the
theory that they are responsible from the very beginning.
They are responsible just according to the law of their unfolding ; not beyond it, a step. Every school is obliged to
go on that theory. You are obliged to conduct a school on
the theory of the steady unfolding of appetency and po-
tency. The old scholastic theology, if imitated by men in
all their relations of life, would destroy the family, make
intercourse and trust impossible, and break up society. The
old theology makes sin to spring from a corrupt nature. I
make it spring from a nature not corrupted, but not unfolded nor harmoniously developed. Both Evolution and
the New Testament show that sin springs from the struggle
for the relative ascendency of animal and spiritual in man's
double nature, and that the conflicts of life are simply the
conflicts between the lower and upper man. We have it in
a dramatic form in the Seventh of Romans, where sin is
regarded as a monster lying in wait for man and attacking
him. Or, changing the idea, one element in the conflict was
the bodily-man, the other was the spiritual-man, and Paul
says in regard to them: "I know that spiritual aspiration and
perception is right; it is holy, it is just, it is good, and with
all my heart I believe in the law of God; but alas! there is
something in me, the law of the flesh, and it is too strong
for the law of the spirit. I see what is good, and I would
do it, but I cannot; I am overthrown in the conflict. When
I would do good, evil is present with me. The good that
I would, I do not; that which I would not, that I do." Is

there a man in this congregation who does not understand that? Is not the Seventh of Romans real—a journalized form of your own experience? Are you not sinful every day of your lives? Going forth with aspirations for the performance of every moral duty, a fountain of benevolence, and coming home stained through and through with conscious selfishness; going out in the morning with the lambent light of love on your brow, and coming back in the evening sullen with hatreds, or quarrels; going out full of power and faith against the temptation of evil, and coming back feeling that you have been soiled by gluttony, by drinking, or by illicit pleasures—pleasure, not duty; pride, not gentleness; self-indulgence, indolence, jealousy, envy—these destroy my purposes, and carry me, like insidious currents, out of the course. Is not this the history of man now; has it not been his history from the beginning? In the development along that middle line where the animal man meets the spiritual man, there is an eternal storm, a cloud that never blows away, and thunder that never dies out of the horizon of time. Is not this confirmed, not only by this generally misunderstood and misinterpreted chapter in Romans, but also by the voice of history; has it not been so from the very beginning?

The race has gained slowly, and with an inconceivable waste. Ages were required to develop morality and the higher moral faculties, mankind meanwhile living more by the force of animal instinct than by reason or conscience. Even after men emerged from barbarism, developed the affections of the household, fortified themselves behind laws and customs, developed institutions, and finally a public sentiment in favor of virtue and religion, they very imperfectly acted upon their knowledge or their consciences. The undertone of daily life in most nations is animal. The "fruits of the Spirit" are yet found in but few, and the whole world is yet a long way from being obedient to the ideals of morality and spirituality which have been developed. Why a benevolent Creator should have chosen such a system, with such an inconceivable waste, with such incomputable delay, with such suffering, is a mystery which

can be solved only in the life beyond. Such a system is
absolutely inconsistent with the conception of benevolence
and of the Fatherhood of God, if one believes that a great
realm of torment subtends this world, and that the contents
of time have been poured into it. It is certain that the vast
majority of the human race have at death been unfit for any
such heaven as is revealed in the New Testament. An un-
sullied heaven could not exist with death, like an Amazon
or Mississippi, pouring into it the soil and dirt of every
latitude along the whole continent of Time. Unless the
human race underwent a sudden elevation, they would reduce the heavenly realm to infinite disorder, and make it
the delta of creation. Analogy would suggest that unfit
men have run their career and perished. The number of
those who hold that immortality is not natural, conferred
on the whole race, but a gift of God to those only who
have attained a sufficient moral development, is increasing;
nor does the language of the New Testament forbid such
a supposition, but encourages it.

The time has come when religious teachers must face
the facts of creation. What has become of the human race
dying through such incomputable periods of time? What
was done for them in this riotous world but to let them
unfold by the slow operation of natural laws, without altar,
teacher, priest, or guide, through ages, that they should be
plunged at death into an infernal torment? Under the conditions in which the world has unfolded, the only acceptable
view would be that the unripe perish. If at death men
have gained in moral elements enough for replanting, we
can believe that they are preserved in some sphere beyond,
growing in a fairer clime and better soil, while those who
have escaped the bondage of the flesh and developed into
likeness to God have the liberty of the sons of God.

It is these considerations that have revolutionized my
educational beliefs. I cannot separate myself from my fellow-men; I cannot content myself with sitting down in a
sweet little parish where everything is regulated by the
highest morality, and where the garden sings with birds,
and where a sweet, loving people fan me with affection,

trust and praise, and then cipher out a doctrine of the sinfulness of man and the reasonableness of eternal punishment. When I think about the condition of men after death, I think of all Africa, and that, too, for thousands of years; I think of all Asia, and that for myriads of years; of every island of the sea; of the population that is for multitude more than the drops of water in the ocean forty times magnified; of that vast sweep of creation, illimitable, uncountable, of human beings that have been created in conditions that imply and necessitate imperfection, and ask myself, What has God done for them all? Where are they? Are they wailing in immitigable torment? If that be so, never let me mention the name of God again. Let me never violate my own nature by calling him " Father." Such a dogma applied to the race through all past time derides, despises, and treads under foot the very foundation ideas which we have of fatherhood. But if we take that away, we have a clean foundation. We may say: Suppose men go out of existence and that is the end of them? Suppose men attain to eternal life through faith in Jesus Christ, in so far as they have unfolded here from animal conditions, and are susceptible of further development in time to come? Or suppose their low moral condition at death brings the experiment to an end ; what has annihilation in it so terrible as the continued existence of unfit natures? What happens when the taper goes out? The earth does not shake. The sun does not stop. Nobody notices it. It simply goes out. And when a man has spent the forces of life here, and has not reached the condition which makes another stage possible to him, suppose he simply goes out? What inhumanity is that, or what shock? He that would live on must live well now; and if he does not begin in his future conditions at the highest point conceivable, he may live high enough up to take a new road and a new start, under better and more favorable circumstances, justifying the wisdom of his having been " subjected *in hope*" to this existence of change and struggle; and in the endless ages of growth, by the " abiding" forces of faith and hope and love, he " shall be delivered from the bondage of corruption into the glorious liberty of the children of God." But as for those that go persistently and steadily lower and lower until they lose the susceptibility and the possibility of human evolution and moral development, suppose the end of the body is the end of life for them? In the great abyss of nothingness there is no groan, no sorrow, no pain, no memory! It is the theory of endless conscious misery of imperfection and wickedness without hope, that accuses the Father-Creator of cruelty.

The old theory of sin, then,—which will be exterminated, I think, by the new light thrown upon the origin of man and the conditions by which the race has been developed,—is repulsive, unreasonable, immoral, and demoralizing. I hate it. I hate it because I love the truth, because I love God, and because I love my fellow-men. The idea that God created the race, and that two of them without experience were put under the temptation of the arch-fiend (or whatever the "creature" was), and that they fell into disobedience to what they did not understand anything about, and that God not only thrust them out of the Garden of Eden, as no parent would ever treat a child in his own household, but that he then transmitted the corruption that was the result of disobedience through the countless ages, and spread it out and out and out, and kept on through the system of nature, mingling damnation on the right and on the left, before and behind—I hate it, because I love God! I abhor it, because I love justice and truth. People say to me, "It is generally understood that you are not a Calvinist." John Calvin can take care of himself. But I am a teacher of righteousness. I am a lover of mankind. It is my business to make the truth, the path in which men's thoughts travel, just as plain as I can, and take out all the obstructions that tend to unbelief. Among the mischievous things of this kind is this whole theory of sin and its origin, that lie at the base of the great evangelical systems of Christianity. I say, it is hideous, it is horrible, it is turning creation into a shambles and God into a slaughterer, and the human race into a condition worse a thousand-fold than that of beasts. The lion is never blamed for being a lion, nor the bear for being a bear, or for being no more than a lion or a bear; nor the horse, nor the swallow, nor the eagle, for not increasing the stature of their being. But man is made to start and not to stop; to go on, and on, and up, and onward, steadily emerging from the controlling power of the physical and animal conditions in which he was born and which enthrall him during his struggle upward, but ever touching higher elements of possibility, and ending in the glorious liberty of the sons of God.

This furnishes a ground of appeal which no man can very well resist. If I say, " You have inherited from Adam a corrupt nature," you may justly rise up and say, " I have not; I inherited from my father and mother as pure a nature as ever descended to a child. There has no drop of Adam's bad blood come through to me." But if I say to you, " God has made man a progressive creature, beginning at the very bottom, on the line of the material, first the animal, then the social, then the intellectual, the æsthetic, the spiritual; and every one of you should live so as to travel on and up; but you have not done it; you are living in the lower portions of your nature; you are not acting becomingly to yourself or your Creator"—if I say this, there is not a man here who can or will deny it. The doctrine of sin, as reflected in the philosophy of Evolution, will carry more power, and have more effect upon the conscience and the aspirations of men, and upon the desires for a higher and better life, than any other. It will explain to them the road by which they are to travel, and the directions they are to take, away from appetites and passions, and will enable them to live more and more perfectly in the higher ranges of emotion and moral sensibility.

The sharp analysis and philosophical refinements which scholastic theology has introduced into the discussion of the origin, nature, and results of sin were unknown to the Old Testament. Sin, there, was concrete; it was evil disposition breaking forth into evil conduct. It was lust, cruelty, gross appetites, and wasteful passions. Among the

legends that are grouped in the earlier portions of Genesis
stands the Garden-Parable of Eden and our first parents.
If treated as a poem, in literature, conveying the simplicity
of the earliest notions of the origin of the Human Family, it
is both harmless and pleasing. If treated as fact, it loses
all its color, and withers as a flower in the desert. If treated
as theology has for a thousand years treated it, it is an
awful morass, out of which have flowed down streams of
mischief, and filled the sphere of religion with dreary and
poisonous influences. There is idyllic beauty in the vision
of a blessed garden inhabited by two ignorant and innocent
beings; the simple story that their wrong-doing led to un-
happpiness and expulsion is a good moral for children.
There let it rest—harmless and even beautiful! There the
whole Old Testament lets it rest! The abomination of
mediæval theology has no existence in the Old Testament.
No priest, lawgiver, or prophet makes this legend a part of
his instruction. The legend dies out. Not once does
Jesus speak of it. In all his reformatory work, in his un-
veiling of the human heart, in his terrible denunciations of
wickedness, he never alludes to Adam, nor to any malign
stream of tendencies flowing from his loins, and carrying
woe to all his posterity. And in that sublime Apocalyptic
Drama, in which the struggle between good and evil, organized into laws, governments, and institutions, is carried
forward with sublime mystical treatment to the final victory
of good, no place is found for Adam, and no place for any
allusion, even, to the malformed and monstrous doctrine of
the fall of the race in Adam, and its alleged terrific con-
sequences, which have become the bed-rock on which
theology has been built. Only Paul touches it. The fall
of Adam and the imputation of his guilt to all his posterity
was a bastard belief of the Jews, grown up, with other
glosses and absurdities of Pharisaic theology, outside of
scriptural authority or teaching; and the apostle, neither
denying nor affirming it, but alluding to it as a theory
familiar to his readers, based upon it the great truth that
Christ brought into life a remedy for all its ills. It was
Christ's moral sufficiency to heal all evil—no matter how it

was supposed to have entered the world, even if through Adam—that was in Paul's heart.

So, then, the Evolutionary philosophy expounds and fortifies the grand requirement on which Christ began his ministry—Repentance. To repent implies universally the need of repentance. That remains; but all those things that have been hinged upon this doctrine, to perplex and to make men revolt from it, will be purged away in the future. We shall simply have a clearer and better view of the indubitable fact that all mankind are sinful; that they need to cease to do evil and learn to do well.

V.

THE NEW BIRTH.

"Jesus answered and said unto him, Verily, verily, I say unto thee, Except a man be born again, he cannot see the kingdom of God."—John iii : 3.

Christ began his ministry where John left off his. "Repent," said John, "for the kingdom of heaven is at hand." Reformation is always the precursor of the higher state, spiritual life; and at that very point Christ took up his teaching, saying: "Repent, for the kingdom of God is at hand." But this was not the end, though it was the beginning. When he fell in with a man of a singularly upright and pure character, Nicodemus,—a true and honorable man, a courageous man in a quiet way, a ruler among the Jews, a man far above immorality or anything of that kind,—to him he said, "You must be born again." Hardly any other character could have been selected where it would have been so little expected that Christ would say, "Even such a one as you must be born again."

I propose to speak on the subject of "Regeneration," and to show how perfectly it fits into that system of nature which the theory of Evolution is supposed to exhibit.

Christ called men from gross and animal life to the moral life; there can be no question about that; he followed thus the whole Old Testament example. That was, however, but a beginning, a foundation on which a noble, invisible, spiritual structure was to be built. He taught that there was a stage yet beyond common morality; that it was possible to unfold man's nature to a higher and

PLYMOUTH CHURCH, SUNDAY MORNING, June 21, 1885. LESSON : John iii.

94

nobler condition; and that man by nature was like a seed
either not planted or not half-grown, and that there was,
beyond mere civic morality—rectitude in ourselves and to
our fellows—even beyond that there was a mighty sphere,
into which every man should go; an ideal character, an
unworldly condition, a heroic devotion to the right; and
that such development was the direct result of divine influence.

Everywhere Jesus illustrated the development of the soul
by the influence of light. The seed is planted in darkness;
it comes forth an immature plant; it steadily unfolds by
the influence of light and heat ; at every stage the plant
is relatively perfect, and yet is preparing for a higher development, but does not reach its final and perfect self
until the last.

The same process of unfolding belongs to man. He is
born an unconscious animal; slowly he develops the senses;
he rises to social sympathies and to will-power. Meantime
intellectual and esthetic growth accompany the general development. Conscience and spiritual susceptibility ripen
latest of all. At each stage of such development the mind
becomes sensitive to higher influences and truths, and finally it is capable of receiving the direct influence of the
divine presence. This is the highest state to which man
may come upon earth. As the touch of a musician brings
differing sounds from the different strings of a harp, so the
divine touch, or inbreathing upon the soul, brings forth
results according to the individual nature of each person.
But the variety, volume, combinations, intensities of the
divine influence upon the souls of different persons is a
theme not yet explored and reduced to knowledge.

Jesus taught that the mind, opened and stimulated by
the divine soul, could bring forth emotions, dispositions,
moral intuitions, joys, and visions such as do not come out
of mere morality, nor out of ordinary influences in secular
life. It was as if he had said: "You know no more about
what you are, undeveloped in the higher possibilities, than a
man knows what the seed is, that stops before it blossoms."

Men begin as animals, go up to the social, come to the

higher range of the esthetic and intellectual, and at last, highest of all, the spiritual, in which they see God, and are in a state of communion with the invisible.

Jesus taught that when one is thus developed his soul reaches up into the sphere where the soul of God, the presence of God, the direct intercourse of his thoughts and emotions with God, are felt; and, still more important, that there comes a state of receptivity of the divine influence, under which the soul has new development and new life. This is not taught once, nor twice, nor casually. Look at the first chapter of this very book of John, the most interior, revelatory book of the whole Bible; the twelfth and thirteenth verses: "But as many as received him, to them gave he power to become the sons of God, even to them that believe on his name: which were born, not of blood, nor of the will of the flesh, nor of the will of man, but of God." Such are in the kingdom of God. He taught that the kingdom of God is not a place; that it is not anything in space or time, with regular organization, rules, instruments, and laws, but a moral condition, and that anybody who reaches up to that moral condition is a member of that kingdom. All those who have their inward and nobler nature developed until they feel in themselves the inspiration of God's presence and love are inhabitants of that kingdom; and none others are.

He taught that all this development prefigures and prepares for a life still beyond this earthly life, when man will enter upon transcendent conditions, which the eye hath not seen, nor the ear heard, nor hath it entered into the heart of man to conceive. Here are the steps and stages, beginning at the lowest and ascending steadily, through the force of material laws, of institutions of instruction, of moral experiences, and the inspiration which comes from God himself, to a state which hovers upon the divine and has not only spiritual intuition, but also spiritual power.

Now in all the realm of creation where evolution is going on, is there any application of it so important, so desirable, so sublime, as this which is figured in Regeneration, or the unfolding process from matter organic and animal to moral, to intellectual and civic, to the final and spiritual, to communion with and unity with God himself?

However variant the philosophy given by theology; whether the "change of heart" results from the human will or the irresistible will of the Spirit; whether through the Truth or by mediation of ordinances; whether it is only reformation or an organic change of faculties; whether it is a sweeping and instantaneous change, a revolution in the government of the faculties or only the first steps of a gradual unfolding,—the grand fact remains that men are capable of reformation, not only of outward conduct, but of inward dispositions, a change which brings the whole man under the control of the reason (Truth), and the moral sense (Conscience), and that by it the opening and ascendency of the spiritual elements of the soul bring men into conscious, personal relations with God.

Nor are we to be repelled by practical mistakes and grotesque experiences, nor by the methods employed to effect a "change of heart," nor by the philosophy applied to the fact of conversion.

What Jesus taught was the absolute necessity, in consequence of universal weakness, ignorance, and sinfulness, the indispensable necessity of some divine power by which man should be lifted out of his animal conditions. He taught in connection with that, also, that this power does exist; that it is a part of that great spiritual province which enfolds this world; that it is open to all men, and that their will is a very important element in it, as respects its possibility.

The Roman Catholic theology is consistent with itself, but almost grotesquely at variance with fact. Baptism of infants relieves them of the guilt of Adam's sin ! As well one might say that education relieves men of the effects of Æsop's Fables. Adam's sin was his own, and no one else's. It never descended. There is none of it in all the world. No immersion, effusion, or sprinkling does any infant need to cleanse from Adam's sin. A single drop is enough for the whole world and for all ages. A microscope of ten-thou-

7

sand million power, in examining the infant soul, could not magnify and bring into vision one single solitary speck of anything that Adam did or did not do. Nothing can be easier than to wash away all that Adam transmitted: and the washing does not do the child any harm. Parents feel as though their children, at the point of death, would be safer if they were only baptized. I pay great respect to that sentiment, because of its many sacred associations, and its consequent power *as* a sentiment. I will baptize any child, whether about to die or promising to live, not because I think it makes the slightest difference with the child, but because I think it would be a great comfort to the parent. I can understand the feeling, to say nothing of having some of it myself: there is something inspiring and helpful to the parent, in the training of a child that has been publicly consecrated to God. But the rite itself, however helpful to the parent, does nothing to the child.

The same is true of adult baptism as a regenerating force. There are thousands who teach that on receiving baptism the soul enters into a new stage, a converted and regenerated stage; and the controversies have run hotly between high and low Episcopacy on that subject, and between Protestantism and Catholicism. But, as a regenerating force, it has no power at all. It is true that when man receives baptism he may have associated with it such ideas of the beginning of the new life that he will bring to bear his own voluntary forces within himself, and from that he may go on higher and better, and so baptism will do him good; but as a priestly act, as a divine power transmitted through the physical ordinance, it has no virtue whatever. It is as innocent as a shadow of a dream.

There can be no mode, however sacred, by which the new birth can be administered officially from without. It is simply a natural part of the unfolding series designed of God in the human constitution; an illustration of that transcendent doctrine, that when a man has unfolded through the lower and intermediate stages, however wise, however useful, however humble, however good, there is in all these things no reason why he should not rise higher, and evolve from those lower preparatory stages into the higher and spiritual stages and instincts of the human mind. Conversion is part and parcel of this grand idea of unfolding.

More than that; not only is regeneration the rising into this higher stage where we come into personal communion with God, but the means by which its attainment has been sought are very largely wise, even in their imperfection. There is nothing in the doctrine of Evolution or in any science surrounding it that has the right to puff out its lips in ridicule at revivals of religion, for they, too, are themselves founded in nature, are philosophical, useful, and in certain stages of the community indispensable. It is true that a child brought up in the nurture and admonition of the Lord may be trained into its spiritual birth gradually and easily, and that probably is the best preparation that could be. The work of adult regeneration is both slow and imperfect; but the training up a child in the way he should go, stage by stage, with the higher light of the Gospel life; the training of a child to right thoughts of God and Christ and love and love of duty, and the whole unfolding process in the sanctuary of the household, is normally best. But alas! where are the priests; where are the parents that either understand it themselves or are qualified to exert such training influences upon their children? How do even so-called Christian households rear men without any such instruction, and without what is more than instruction, training;—for to instruct is to give knowledge; training reduces knowledge to conduct. How few are the families that reduce the instruction of their children to such habits and such results that the children grow up unto the Lord from the cradle! I believe that will take place in the latter-day glory. I believe that household instruction will yet supersede all other forms of moral influence; but, taking facts as they are, there is a second, though less perfect way, namely, bringing to bear upon adult communities influences that shall enable men to rise, under (I had almost said) an atmospheric influence, to change the current, to exalt the life.

Many men have ridiculed revivals, and even good men have looked askance upon them, as being of human device, and have pointed out all their defects and miscarriages, and have frequently brought them into contempt. But they are founded on a natural law, and a beneficent one. Community of feeling among large companies is favorable to the development of each individual in the line in which that feeling is moving. This is the law of life; it is the law of civilization; and it grows more and more subdivided—that is, it is applied more perfectly to every element in human life as civilization advances. Over and above the individual power of the man's will is the collective power in which he floats, of the wills of all those round about him. Business avails itself of this. Men have substituted a modern word for prosperity; it is called a "business boom"—and a boom, I suppose, is where after comparatively shallow channels there is snow melted in the mountain or running off the hills, and the river fills up its channels, and comes rushing down with irresistible power, sweeping everything before its current. There is what is called a business boom, a general influence, by the contributive feeling of multitudes of men. It may be in one channel of business, it may be in another; it may be in many. It may be so broad as to cover the whole continent, and every man knows how easy it is to do business then. How alert, how sagacious, how efficient he is! On the other hand, when the market runs low and slack, how hard it is for a man to crowd himself individually up to that point of enterprise that he reaches when business is "lively," as it is called!

Such was the initial popular movement in which the great Protestant Reformation of the sixteenth century took place; such was the Reformation itself, though mixed up with political considerations and vastly also with theological controversies and despotisms and ambitions. Nevertheless the root and substance of the great Reformation of ecclesiastical religion was a revival of intellectual life and of moral feeling among large masses of men.

So is it in amusements of every kind. Every year shows

new forms; and, not merely by the habit of imitation, but by those subtle and invisible influences which spring from the desire and thought and feeling of thousands, more than from the thought of one, amusements thrive; this kind to-day and that kind to-morrow. So is it with friendship, sociality, with pleasure in households, and enjoyments of every kind. There are periods of winter when everything is solid and stolid. There are periods of thawing out, when the sun of friendship and social life seems to bring every-day warmth to the natures of men. It is the very law of the unfolding of civilization, taking on sometimes one form, sometimes another.

Now, when religious sentiment itself comes in its turn to that great possibility, namely, the increment of moral impulse, discernment, purposes, by the concurrent sympathy and movement of hundreds and of thousands in revivals, is it to be ridiculed and to be put away? It is the highest form which this movement ever takes, it is the highest and noblest. Not a single reason can there be why there should not be revivals of religion.

A single candle throws light to one man who reads, and only one. A hundred candles give light to every man in the house. A single stick does not create much warmth; a fagot more; a bonfire more yet; and a furnace melts all things in its glow and heat. A single penitent thought limps ; a thousand men, all of them feeling the pressure of wrongdoing in the past, and the desire for elevation and inspiration, reflect their feeling one upon the other, and it becomes easy for each to do that which it would otherwise be almost impossible to do.

The wisdom of the church is seen at such times as these, when meetings are multiplied and things are discoursed on for instruction which are most likely to give man a higher view of his destiny and his duty; when the feelings are touched by sweet songs addressed to them; when the imagination itself glows as the stars that make the night shine. And when all these things are brought to bear, how normal and philosophical is the operation of the law of revivals! Here you have the logical stages: man is to be regarded as universally sinful, that is, he is living in his lower life, and needs to be unfolded; next comes the doctrine that it is possible to unfold a man through all the stages onward and upward till you come to the spiritual, in which the higher qualities of reason, imagination and moral sentiment predominate absolutely; and here are the instruments by which men help themselves in their various emergencies to that higher possibility.

Revivals of religion and all kinds of religious service in churches, that melt, lift, and inspire men to a higher life, are normal. No science is going to abolish them. You might as well put icicles under your kettle to get boiling water, as to put scientific problems about electricity under the church to get lukewarmness boiling and evaporating.

The teaching of the Scripture is that all men are dead in trespasses and in sin; that the spiritual part of them is overwhelmed. They are dead. If they are undeveloped in any part, that part is dead. If even they are not grossly sinful, if they are unsprouting and undeveloped, every such part as lingers it may be said has not yet come unto life. It is figuratively said to be dead. That is the condition of the human race. The vast majority of them are little more than animals to-day, and the civilized and religious portions of the globe have crept up slowly, and are very little higher. The penetrating, energizing influences of the higher class of religious people are but in the twilight of the highest stage. Men are dead. Their life lies farther beyond them than they know: for it is higher than they know; for it is other than they know. They are living as to the body, and as to matter, and as to lower society; but as to that which is vastly greater and unmeasured,—God and spiritual being, and immortality and eternity,—men are not alive; they are dead to those things. To the blind man the whole world is obliterated. To the deaf man there is no sound in the air by day or by night. All things are dead where there is no spiritual apprehension.

In unwrapping a mummy three thousand years old, wheat was found. The gums had preserved its vitality three thousand years. There was a crop of wheat lying in the cerements of that old mummy, and when the ancient grain was brought out and planted—O, the miracle of Nature! It threw down the root, it lifted up the stem, it grew and came to the sickle and was reaped; and that very wheat has its posterity in many of our fields to-day. It was dead; but not deader than those men are who, in the cerements of their lower life, have yet the germs of the higher life wrapped up and unsprouting. To them comes neither moisture, nor air, nor heat, nor life. They are dead.

There are multitudes that are like my Wisteria: a plant of the loveliest habit, which you shall see in the early spring abundantly, in the cities and in the country. When transplanted it is very apt to be obstinate and to refuse to grow. I planted it early, and I got a little dwarf, stumpy vine, tree-like, not two feet high. I waited one year, two years, three years, four years, until I got out of all patience with it, and I said to the gardener, "Take it up; throw it away." He took it up, but not to throw it away. He planted it in a more favorable corner, where something happened, I know not what, in the mystery of Nature, and the very next year it broke its bonds and sent up its vine, and clasped and clambered and covered all the end of the house, and ran up on to the adjacent trees, and filled the whole air with its perfume and with the beauty of its blossom. Multitudes of men there are just like it, living so near the ground, and without any aspiration, that they never know what they are, in themselves, and to what their possibilities lead up—never.

This figure runs all through the Bible. What more could I have done? What more could have been done to my vineyard, saith the Lord, than I have done? yet when I looked for grapes brought it forth wild grapes. I planted it, I nourished it, I had a right to the highest fruit, and I get nothing but wildings. Christ himself gives this thought in a parabolic form in one of his miracles where he saw the tree that brought not forth figs, and he said, "Henceforth let nothing grow on it." It did not yield figs as it should; it was undeveloped. And again he said: "I am the true vine, ye are the branches; any branch in me that beareth not fruit, he taketh away; or if it beareth a little, he pruneth it so that it shall bear more fruit." That idea of the unfolding sequence and series in human nature, the idea of fruit, is expressed in the Old Testament and in the New, with endless variety and with effulgent beauty.

In the views thus far expounded I remark, first, that the executive doctrines hitherto employed by the churches rest upon a basis of fact, and are not overthrown but are confirmed by the revelations of science. What are the executive doctrines? They are the doctrines that, in the providence of God, are designed to stimulate and develop human nature, and bring it up from its lowest stage to the highest. They are fundamental. Fundamental doctrines in systematic theology are those that are necessary to any given system. A chain must have every link in every link. If it be Calvinism that you are speaking of, then there are certain doctrines indispensable to that system. If it be Arminianism, then there must be certain foundation-doctrines on which that system is built. But the fundamental doctrines of Christianity are those that have a tendency in them to stimulate, and develop, and spiritualize. They are the doctrines that teach man his infirmity and his sinfulness. Jesus hardly taught but assumed the universal sinfulness of man. There was no need of argument or even of statement. He might just as well have taught them that there was such a thing as rain, and that rain was wet. It is every man's consciousness that the human race and everything in it are deficient morally, and are not to be measured with any satisfaction upon any higher ideal. Therefore the Gospel has assumed this as its basis, the very thing on which Christ went forth, as John before him did, saying, "Repent." Why, but for the universal sinfulness of man? That sinfulness is not any of Adam's crime or ichor, not sinfulness after this, that, or the other theory, but the undoubted fact that men are living in their lower and animal selves; sinfulness is the outpouring upon society of the passions, the appetites, the selfishness, the pride, the cruelty—everything that belongs to the lower life of men. Mankind universally believe in it, and mostly with despairing and without looking for any remedy. The doctrine of the sinfulness of man is indisputable, and it grows more and more certain to the consciousness of men the clearer the light is that you bring to bear upon it, and the higher the standards that you bring wherewith to measure it.

Then, we have the fact that out of this lower life there is an ascending process by which men may come to a stage so much higher than their lower physical stage that it is called a "New Life." It is to human life what the fire is to the candle, it is the bright consuming flame sending out light on every side, though it is dependent upon the inferior candle for its light and development. The doctrine of regeneration implies, on the one side, despair by reason of our helplessness, and on the other side, according to the Scriptures, courage and hope. The doctrine taught abundantly—especially in John, more than anywhere else I think—that the Spirit helpeth our infirmities, as the Apostle says; the doctrine that Christ was the light of the world; that he came to give health to the world; that there is such a thing as merging our life into his life; and that we should come up to this highest state of blessedness, which belongs to the kingdom of heaven—this doctrine of our religion knocks against no doctrine of philosophy, but is in perfect concord with them. The doctrine of the reality of holiness in this life,—I do not mean absolute perfection, but the life bodily in a spiritual freedom rather than in the animal freedom of half-developed human life,— this is taught too. These four truths—the fact of sinfulness; the fact of regeneration, its need, its reality, its possibility; the life-giving Spirit of God, that helps a man out of this lower into the higher stage; and the fact of the holiness into which man may come by the aid of the Spirit, concurrent with his own will—these are what I call the executive doctrines of Christianity; and if these are faithfully preached in simplicity and earnestness by any man, he can scarcely fail of the fruit of such preaching. The particular doctrine which this discourse is intended to show that Evolution assumes and establishes, is *Regeneration.*

That is my theology; it is a working theology. I believe

a good many things besides, and I suspect a good many things which I do not yet say I believe. There are a thousand things in the Word of God that our philosophy never dreamed of, new as well as old. But this—the need of every man, and the provision for that need in Jesus Christ, the help of the Holy Ghost, the reality of all that higher character which ranks a man as a citizen of the kingdom of heaven—this is my practical theology, that I always have preached and always shall.

I look back now upon nearly forty years' ministry here, and see what the fruit has been. It has not been as large and as good as it would have been if you had had a better fruiterer. But I am not unwilling to compare with others the men and women that have grown up under my preaching, their development in nobleness, their cheer, their hopefulness, their courage, their kindness, their lovableness, and their self-denial, which ceases to be self-denial because they learn to love working for others. I think I am not apt to be proud, but I may thank God that I have the test before me in hundreds and in thousands that the word preached by me has been blessed, not simply to the hope of their final salvation, but to their present evolution into higher, statelier, more beautiful, attractive, winning souls.

Any man that preaches these doctrines and sticks to them, and carries men up, must be orthodox. That is what Christ came for. That is what the Holy Spirit is given out for. A man's belief about what the future condition of things will be, may or may not be important. But as to the sinfulness of men, the need of regeneration, the reality of the change of heart, the divine influence to help every man up and on, and the final completion of character on that high spiritual basis—whoever believes in these things and in this simple creed is equipped to do the Lord's work; and you have no right to exclude him. I know that men say, one has no right to remain in a church when he does not believe in all the rules and regulations of it. I reply that no church has a right to exist with rules and regulations such that a true Christian man cannot dwell in it. If he does not believe what the church teaches about baptism, he is not bound to go out of the church, but churches are bound to change—not their beliefs but their rules—for the sake of keeping every one in whom Christ has received, the evidence of which is made plain by a godly life. If he doubts the Apostolic succession, he is not bound to go out of that church if he has been brought up in it. Christ's church must be so constructed that whoever loves God and man and devotes the power of his life to men's welfare, shall be undisturbed in it.

It is said that men who are going to be preachers and teachers, and expect to have the indorsement of the ecclesiastical authorities, must give the ground upon which they are going to teach. A man should give this answer to that matter: " I believe all the world is involved in sin; I believe Jesus Christ came to redeem men from their sins; I believe that he taught that there was a power given forth in answer to faith and prayer and praise, by which the Holy Ghost should lift a man up into the higher realm of his nature, and give him ascendency and permanency there. I do believe that it is possible for a man, regenerated and lifted up, to come to that knowledge and that communion of faith by which God is his companion night and day and everywhere. I do believe that when a man has otherwise the mental conception, the physical constitution, the strength, the organization, and is inspired of God, he may become gifted with insight and foresight, and may have more than that, the power of working something that looks very much like miracles. I believe in the theology that stands directly connected with the discipline, the development, and the perfection of the human race." If, besides all that, the church wants to carry baggage and baggage-wagons, and all sorts of furniture and all sorts of ordnance, and is able to do so, it may. There is no law by which a man should not go to battle now with Saul's armor on, but he would be a fool to sweat under Saul's armor on a midsummer's day. So that all of the churches or the people may be just as foolish as they please, if they do not set themselves up for models, and if they do not command all others to imitate them, or else exorcise them because they are out of the path of faith.

Finally, let me not leave this subject argumentatively, or controversially. May I not say to every person here that your own consciousness teaches you that you are living in a low and sinful and undeveloped state? I do not ask you to go back to the creed or the confession; I ask your own consciousness, Do you not know you are living low, selfish, carnal lives? Does not the strength of your life run in the lower channels of it? I ask every man here, Do you not believe that you need to be elevated to a higher stage; and if there is such a thing as a divine in-spiring influence, do you not desire that that influence may lift you up out of your carnal state into a spiritual state; and ought you not to be glad of it, that you may be born again, and not groan, as if it were putting a great burden and task of duty upon you? Ought you not—as men who are shut up in a dungeon and have groped around and finally found a door that opens out into the light through which you may escape—ought you not to say, "Blessed be God that I may be born again"? Ought not every man to be ashamed to live in the dull and lower elements of possi-ble being when perfection is ready and is waiting for him? Do not count yourselves unworthy of that life which God imparts to those that rise up into communion with Him!

I beseech you, then, to understand that this doctrine of man's sinfulness and need of change and possible develop-ment is found not only in the text of the Bible; nor does it stand simply in any ecclesiastical schemes which men have built up: it stands fully bottomed on the indubitable facts of God's revelation in nature. Evolution is laying the ground, I believe, for more powerful revivals of religion in the days which are yet to come, for more facile changes in men from below upward, than ever have been known in the days that have gone by. May God speed the time!

VI.

DIVINE PROVIDENCE AND DESIGN.

" To whom will ye liken me, and make me equal, and compare me, that we may be like ?"—Isa. xlvi : 5.

There is no attempt in the Hebrew Scriptures to give definite form to God, nor strict analysis, nor any comprehensive theory; as we formulate in modern times "the philosophy of things," there is no philosophy of God made known in the Bible,—any more than there is science in nature. Science is the recognition by men of things pre-existing in the world of matter; and theologies are the consciousness and the intellectual views of men respecting the facts that are set forth in the Bible. It was expressly forbidden, indeed, that there should be any form given to God in carved statues. They were not to be allowed to make images, and the spirit of the command is equally strong against pictures and against fashioning in the imagination any definite conception of form. It degrades God in the mind and imagination of men to limit him by forms of matter. There is, to be sure, addressed not to the senses but to the imagination, some form given to God by descriptions—Isaiah, Daniel, John, the Apocalyptic writer; yet even then there was but sublime indefiniteness. There was the declaration of will, the quality of disposition, the attributes of power and of glory; but they were all diffused through time and space, and with no definite outlines. The "word-pictures" in Isaiah and Daniel and the Revelation of John, though descriptions, are symbols and figures playing on the imagination; which if at once

PLYMOUTH CHURCH, Sunday Morning, June 28, 1885. LESSON : Matthew vi : 25-34.

109

reduced by art to definite form, not only lose all their beauty, but are worse than grotesque—they are ridiculous, as any man may see on looking at Van Eyck's pictures—of the Flemish school—of the Lamb with seven eyes and ten horns, holding something in his split hoof, which represents the hand. Indeed, even as a symbol and imaginatively considered, it is all we can do to read those figures of the prophets and the Apocalyptic writer; but to reduce them to absolute form is preposterous. And the same thing we see in literature. The Ariels and the witches of Shakespeare are charming and striking when they are read, but ridiculous when they are acted. The conception is so subtile, and belongs to so tenuous an atmosphere, that we cannot bear it in flesh and blood form. Personality, however, running through every phase of human knowledge,—purposes, persuasive force, emotion with tides and moods, decrees, foresights, control, design, providence special and universal, together with the fountains of feeling from which spring all those affections and all those heroic dispositions which the whole world worships in its great men—these are all Scriptural revelations of God; always the Biblical development of God, which conforms to the fact of infinity, and to the unsearchable in time and in space. It is, then, remarkable that the process of scientific unfolding finds itself in close analogy with this mode of treatment of the divine Being. Men think that if theology should change its whole method,—which made up God on an arithmetical plan, and exactly described all his attributes, and located them and their functions, and articulated every part until they had fashioned a complete mechanical and imaginary God,—if anything should change the idea of God in the popular mind and render it more simple and less searchable, that must be wandering away from the truth. But it is going back toward the truth—going back toward the divine nature. Any formulation of the divine nature, which becomes definite, crystalline, philosophic, is a perpetual affront to the method of God's revelation, whether in Scripture or in science.

Science, at length, is tending to relieve the world of the

idealizations of the Greek philosophy and of the hard and organic materialism of the Roman mind; also of the ignorant analyses and quibbling refinements of the schoolmen of Mediæval ages. It is not without reason, then, that Christian men have looked upon the tendency of science to destroy the beliefs of men in certain fundamental notions of God, with apprehension and alarm.

The theory of Design has been supposed to be overthrown by the inevitable tendencies of science. The existence of a general and special Providence of God has been supposed to be incompatible with the deductions of science. The scope and use of Prayer have been ridiculed by some votaries of science. The apparent scientific denial of the possibility of Miracles—ending in the impossibility of that greatest of all, the incarnation of Jesus Christ—all these have troubled men of faith without any just reason.

It will be my design this morning, therefore, to discuss at least two of these matters—the question of Design in creation and the question of a general and a special Providence, as they stand related, not to the Scriptural testimony alone, but to what we now know of the course of natural law in this world.

The atheistic view—that is, the view taken by Haeckel (one of the ablest scientists of Germany, though not altogether the safest in generalizations)—the view that this world needs no God, that it has in itself provision for all the phenomena which have taken place—instead of simplifying matters and relieving us, makes matters still more difficult to comprehend.

Atheism taxes credulity a great deal more than even the most superstitious notions do. There is nothing in human experience which can furnish a basis for believing the origin and the progress of the world of its own self without any external influence. Time and matter being given and certain forces established, then the world, to be sure, could be unfolded as it is taught by Evolution; but where was the matter and where were the laws that directed it through uncountable periods, and gave to it system, progress, direction not only, but organic symmetry? No man can believe that things happen of themselves. There is always a force prior to an effect, and that fact is wrought into the very (I had almost said) common-sense of mankind. But the origin of matter, and what matter is, we do not know any better than we do what the spirit is, the mind, the soul. We are absolutely ignorant of what matter is. You can tell what forms matter takes, what functions it performs, but what it is, in and of itself, no man can tell.

The men that ridicule the doctrine of the soul or spirit as something separate from matter, and defy an intelligent definition of it, are no better off in their mud than we are in our mire. The origin of matter, the existence of tendencies or laws in matter, of itself, is simply inconceivable.

The law of cause and effect is fundamental to the very existence of science, and, I had almost said, to the very operation of the human mind. So, then, we gain nothing by excluding divine intelligence, and to include it smooths the way to investigation, and is agreeable to the nature of the human mind. It is easier to conceive of the personal divine being with intelligence, will and power, than it is to conceive of a world of such vast and varied substance as this, performing all the functions of intelligence and will and power. That would be giving to miscellaneous matter the attributes which we denied to a personal God.

The doctrine of Evolution, at first sight, seems to destroy the theory of intelligent design in creation, and in its earlier stages left those who investigated it very doubtful whether there was anything in creation but matter, or whether there was a knowable God.

So sprang up the Agnostic school, which includes in it some of the noblest spirits of our day. "God may exist, but we do not know it." That is what the Bible says from beginning to end; that is what philosophy is now beginning to explain. We cannot understand the divine nature, so exalted above everything that has yet been developed in human consciousness, except it dawns upon us when we are ourselves unfolding, and rising to such a higher operation of our own minds as does not belong to the great mass of the human race. God is to be seen only by those faculties that verge upon the divine nature, and to them only when they are in a state of exaltation. Moral intuitions are not absolute revelations, but they are as sure of higher truths as the physical senses are of material truths.

But the question of design in creation, which has been a stable argument for the proof of the existence of God and his attributes, seems to have been shaken from its former basis. It is being restored in a larger and grander way, which only places the fact upon a wider space, and makes the outcome more wonderful. Special creation, and the adaptation in consequence of it, of structure to uses in animals, and in the vegetable kingdom to their surroundings, has always been an element of God's work regarded as most remarkable. How things fit to their places! how regular all the subordinations and developments that are going on! how fit they are to succeed one another! Now the old theory conceived God as creating things for special uses. When the idea of the lily dawned on him, he smiled and said: "I will make it;" and he made it to be just as beautiful as it is. And when the rose was to be added, like an artist God thought just how it should be all the way through. That is the old view—that some plants were made to do without water and could live in parched sands; and that some could live only in the tropics; and thus God adapted all his creation to the climate and the soil and the circumstances, and it was a beautiful thing to see how things did fit, by the divine wisdom, the places where they were found.

Then comes Evolution and teaches that God created through the mediation of natural laws; that creation, in whole or detail, was a process of slow growth, and not an instantaneous process; that plants and animals alike were affected by their surrounding circumstances favorably or unfavorably; and that, in the long-run, those which were best adapted to their environment survived, and those perished which could not adapt themselves to the conditions of soil, climate, moisture, cold or heat which in the immeasurable periods of creation befell them. The adaptation then of plants to their condition did not arise from the

8

direct command of the **Great Gardener**; but from the fact that, among these infinite gradations of plants, only those survived and propagated themselves which were able to bear the climate and soil in which they found themselves; all others dwindled and perished. Of course there would be a fine adjustment of the plant to its condition; it came to this by a long preparation of ancestral influences.

How beautiful it is to see a plant growing right under the cheek of a precipice or a snow-bed, or by the edges of winter through the year! Men say how beautiful the thought was that God should create life in vegetables and flowers right alongside the snow, as it were, to cheer the bosom of winter: whereas it turned out that everything that could not live there died; and, by and by, there were some plants so tough that they could live there, and they did; and the adaptation was the remainder after a long series of perishings. Men say, What a remarkable instance of divine design that the cactus can live on arid deserts, where water scarcely falls more than once or twice a year; and what a special creation and adaptation it was on the part of God that he should make such plants as that! But the Evolutionist says that all the plants were killed in succession until it came about, in the endless variations of the vegetable kingdom, that a plant developed whose structure was covered, as it were, with an india-rubber skin, and whose leaves were substantially little cisterns, which drank up all the water they wanted to use through the summer, and so continued to live in spite of their dry surroundings, when others could not live because they could not adapt themselves. So the argument for special design, as we used to hold it, fails there.

Through long periods all things tended to vary more or less from their original forms, and adapted themselves to their necessary conditions; and what could not do this perished; for the theory of Evolution is as much a theory of destruction and degradation as of development and building up. As the carpenter has numberless shavings, and a vast amount of wastage of every log which he would shape to some use, so creation has been an enormous waste, such as seems like squandering, on the scale of human life, but not to Him that dwells in Eternity. In bringing the world to its present conditions, vast amounts of things have lived for a time and were unable to hold on, and let go and perished. We behold the onflowing, through immeasurable ages of creation, of this peculiar tendency to vary, and in some cases to improve. The improvement is transmitted; and in the battle of life, one thing conflicting with another, the strong or the best adapted crowd out the weak, and these continue to transmit their qualities until something better yet shall supplant them.

Vast waste and the perishing of unfit things is one of the most striking facts in the existence of this world ; for while life is the consummation, death seems to be the instrument by which life itself is supplied with improvement and advancement. Death prepares the way for life. Things are adapted thus to their condition, to their climate, to their food; or by their power of escape from their adversaries, or their power of establishing themselves and of defending their position, they make it secure. The vast universe, looked at largely, is moving onward and upward in determinate lines and directions, while on the way the weak are perishing. Yet, there is an unfolding process that is carrying creation up to higher planes and upon higher lines, reaching more complicated conditions in structure, in function, in adaptation, with systematic and harmonious results, so that the whole physical creation is organizing itself for a sublime march toward perfectness.

If single acts would evince design, how much more a vast universe, that by inherent laws gradually builded itself, and then created its own plants and animals, a universe so adjusted that it left by the way the poorest things, and steadily wrought toward more complex, ingenious, and beautiful results ! Who designed this mighty machine, created matter, gave to it its laws, and impressed upon it that tendency which has brought forth the almost infinite results on the globe, and wrought them into a perfect system ? Design by wholesale is grander than design by retail.

You are all familiar with the famous illustration of Dr. Paley, where a man finds a watch, and infers irresistibly that that watch was made by some skillful, thoughtful watch-maker. Suppose that a man, having found a watch, should say to himself, "Somebody thought this out, somebody created this ; it is evidently constructed and adapted exactly to the end in view—the keeping of time." Suppose, then, that some one should take him to Waltham, and introduce him into that vast watch-factory, where watches are created in hundreds of thousands by machinery ; and suppose the question should be put to him, "What do you think, then, about the man who created this machinery, which of itself goes on cutting out wheels, and springs, and pinions, and everything that belongs to making a watch? If it be an argument of design that a man could make one watch, is it not a sublimer argument of design that there is a man existing who could create a manufactory turning out millions of watches, and by machinery too, so that the human hand has little to do but to adjust the parts already created by machines ?" If it be evidence of design in creation that God adapted one single flower to its place and functions, is it not greater evidence if there is a system of such adaptations going on from eternity to eternity ? Is not the Creator of the system a more sublime designer than the creator of any single act?

Or, let me put down before you an oriental rug, which we all know has been woven by women squatting upon the ground, each one putting in the color that was wanted to form the figure, carrying out the whole with oriental harmony of color. Looking upon that, you could not help saying, "Well, that is a beautiful design, and these are skillful women that made it, there can be no question about that." But now behold the power-loom, where not simply a rug with long, drudging work by hand is being created, but where the machine is creating carpets in endless lengths, with birds, and insects, and flowers, and scrolls, and every element of beauty. It is all being done without a hand touching it. Once start the engine, and put the perforated papers above the loom, and that machine turns out a carpet that puts to shame the beauty of these oriental rugs. Now the question is this: Is it an evidence of design in these women that they turn out such work, and is it not evidence of a higher design in the man who turned out that machine —that loom—which could carry on this work a thousand-fold more magnificently than human fingers did?

It may be safely said, then, that Evolution, instead of obliterating the evidence of divine Design, has lifted it to a higher plane, and made it more sublime than it ever was contemplated to be under the old reasonings.

Next, it has been thought that science, by introducing the doctrine of the universality and invariableness of law, and giving it a larger and a more definite field of operation, destroys all possibility of a special Providence of God over men and events. It has been said that everything that we know anything about in this world has happened by the force of law, and that it is not likely that God will turn law aside or change law and interject his immediate creative will for the sake of any favorites that he has in this world. I need hardly say to you, after the reading of the passage (Matt. vi : 19–34) this morning in our opening services, that no doctrine is taught more explicitly by the Lord Jesus Christ than this doctrine of the personal watch and care of God over men and things,—that nothing happens without his inspection. The theist admits that there may be a general Providence supervising the machinery of the universe. But the Christian doctrine of special Providence,—the adaptation of all the forms of nature to the welfare of particular individuals, races and nations,—if this doctrine of Providence were to be overthrown by science, I need not say that it would make a very great breach in our faith, in the New Testament and as to the divinity of Christ himself. One of the things that makes life endurable is that we are not like so many stones, rolled, broken and rattling down by violent torrents, without any particular force of design; but that we are grouped together in communities and in families ; and, as individuals, under the beneficent inspection of God, who has a continual thought of our welfare. The world would seem to me a very dreary place if I did not believe in the immanence of the divine Mind and the interference of the divine Will. The belief in a special divine Providence brings with it great peace and confidence, and is exactly suited to the ignorance and helpless condition of the human race. A chariot with no driver, an engine with no engineer, a voyage and no captain or officers, a raging battle and no commander —what would all these events be in comparison with undirected human life upon this whirling globe, in its endless passage through time? The world is full of ignorance, disease, revolution, wars, pestilence, and immeasurable disasters. They spring from definite laws; but laws are cruel to those who are too ignorant to obey them. All this does not establish the doctrine of a divine special Providence, but it makes it devoutly to be wished that such a government may be proved to exist. It should make one very unwilling to destroy the teaching of Jesus and thus reduce the world to orphanage.

But is there any *reason* in the doctrine of a Natural Law which controls all things, and no God who controls law itself? It is said that a special divine Providence implies an interference with the regular action of natural laws; a direct exercise of the divine will aside from or even opposed to their uniform operation ; that it is not philosophical to suppose that God shows partiality—that he sets aside for some men the laws which regulate the conduct of others ; that he favors particular persons, families, and nations. It is said also that God works only through laws and never sets them aside. But this is begging the question. What are natural laws? In the lower elements of creation they may be described as the behavior of matter. Under the same conditions, matter, so far as we know, behaves in the same manner. What the compelling influence is that produces uniform sequences to certain antecedents, we do not know. We can conceive of a Being from whom goes forth an energy, generic and unconscious, quite aside from conscious will and purpose. To a limited extent this condition exists in man. Men call it magnetic force, or personal atmosphere. We can imagine that as the sun fills the world with light and heat, not by any volition, but by the nature given to it by God, so there may be in God himself a radiancy of power separable from thought or purpose, and which fills the universe with the energy that men call Force or Natural Law. But to say that God's will never interferes with this ordinary effluence of force, to control or direct, is an assumption of knowledge which no man can possess. Using the term Law, for convenience in its popular sense, as a ruling and uniform action of force inherent in matter and pervading creation, it may be pointed out, that, while the inorganic materials of creation are held in the grasp of law with the greatest constancy, yet, as matter rises upon the scale through mechanical, chemical forces to organic life, and again from the lower forms of life to higher organization, the forces and their laws become more complex and diversified. What are called laws of nature seem to occupy, among the lower conditions of matter, the place of mind in higher animals and in the human family. But as the human mind rises in the scale it gives evidence of more and more control over the laws of matter; and this fact seems to suggest the possibility that the mind, in its highest development, is of all natural forces itself the greatest and most universally active and efficient.

But, leaving this suggestion, there can be no doubt of the control which the human mind exercises over those forces which men call natural laws. The popular idea is, and it is partaken of very largely by philosophical men, that laws are unchangeable, irresistible in their sphere, that they are not to be controlled, and that they compel all. It is felt as though they were great energies that moved as bars of steel would move through crowds, overturning, bruising and destroying all that came in their way. The irresistibleness of natural law is an illusion. Of all the things within the conception of the imagination, there is nothing gentler, nothing more pliable, nothing more applicable, nothing more controllable, than natural physical laws. They are a great deal more like the silk thread than

they are like the needle that carries it, or than they are
like a bar of iron or steel.   Only obey a natural law, and
it becomes your servant; you must break yourself in as
you would a steed, whose broad back then carries you
whithersoever you will.

Natural laws are constantly checked, constantly contra-
dicted and made inoperative.   They are set in conflict
one against the other.   The laws of chemical affinity are
perpetually thwarted in the laboratory.   The acid cannot
have its way when it meets with an alkali, or the alkali
when it meets an acid; they make a compromise.   In me-
chanics the law of gravity cannot pull down the stone which
you put an iron pillar under to support.   In its wildness and
untouched condition every weight must fall to the ground,
but you say to the law of gravity, "You shall not pull that
stone down."   You have propped it up and made it resist
the operation of gravity.   Everywhere throughout the world
you can put law against law, and you can make a compromise not only, but you can make laws do, by the infusion
of human reason and human will, that which they would
never do of themselves.   That is the root and fundamental
quality of civilization, that at last large communities have
gained such a knowledge of natural laws that they have
harnessed them and drive them for all work everywhere.

Laws depend upon human intelligence for their achievements.   In their wildest state natural laws are only half
fruitful.   Winds have roamed like wild giants over the
globe, roaring hither and thither, before there was a human
population; but now they grind the food of man by turning
windmills, or swell the sails that carry men for all their
purposes round and round the world.   The wild wind that
knew no master is apprenticed to ten thousand masters
to-day.   Human reason has taken possession of it and made
it work for its living.   Water floated in the clouds or stormed
on the sea, or rushed forth in useless rivers.   It, too, has
been reduced to service, everywhere turning wheels, everywhere replenishing the supplies of society through the
medium of manufactories; and even in the desert, by irri-
gation, making the wilderness to bud and blossom as the

rose. Water had never done that of itself; water inspired by human will does it.

Electricity, the great buffoon of the North in winter nights, flashes, too, in storms,—the pyrotechnist of the world. But to-day it is subdued. Now, shut up in boxes, it heals the sick. It lights our streets and dwellings. It plays post-boy and carries news in the twinkling of an eye around the whole world. In its early day, untouched by the will of man, what did the electric element do? It was worthless, barren, fruitless, or fruitful only of harm to the works of man; and it became very fruitful to all functions of good simply because the will of man learned to utilize it.

Not by violating, either, but by *using* the laws of nature, men can and do create a providence; and thus we come back to the gist of the matter. I can use the laws of nature so that they shall be a providence to me, and I can use them so that they shall be a providence to my family. It is by the use of natural laws, not by violating them, by harnessing them and making them work, that I can make my family respectable and send out my children to the vocations of life. A man that is a drunkard or a man that is a knave cannot bless his children thus; but, on the other hand, a wise man, a patient man, a skillful man, an industrious man, can make all the difference between poverty and distress on the one side, and eminence and wealth and prosperity on the other side, by the use of natural law,—not by violating it, but by using it.

Not only can a man take care of himself and of his household, but of all his neighbors as well. He can impart the benefit of his knowledge to his whole neighborhood. Surely, God ought to be able to do almost as much as that in the wider use of natural law!

One single combination of laws in a machine revolutionizes the industry of the globe. It gives to the poor man what before only the princely loom gave to the rich sovereigns of the earth; and a man's invention of a machine made cotton the fabric of the world, on whose existence statesmanship turned and nations lived and throve, or perished. A man can, by discoveries of the functions of natural law, bless the age in which he lives. What are the steamboats that ply the world around, what are the factories that are turning out wondrous things for the whole population of the globe, and what is the world itself but a wise subjugation of natural laws by human intelligence directed by the human will?

If, then, God cannot create a providence by using, not violating, natural laws, he cannot do what the meanest creatures on earth can do in some degree and measure. All the talk about the inevitableness of natural laws and their being utterly irresistible is inconsiderate and unfounded. He can use these laws without violating them, just as men use them. He can exert, directly or indirectly, upon the consciousness of men, an influence which shall make them enactors of his decree. Theists recognize a general Providence, by which the world and all its laws and apparatus are preserved and kept in working order. But Jesus taught more than this; he taught that God uses the machinery of the world for his own special ends. It does not follow that God overrides stated forces; he can, with superior skill, direct the great powers of Nature to special results. God's will, or mind, may be supposed to act upon the human mind, either through ordinary laws, or directly, without any intermediate instruments.

In the case of direct influence the effect may be supposed to be an exaltation of the whole mind or of special parts of it. The result would be not merely a quickening of faculties, but an exaltation of the mind to a higher plane, on or around which play new energies or forces; and to this superior condition of mind there would be easily opened new vision, new powers—especially the power to more wisely adapt, direct, and use natural laws, even those which pertain to the higher planes.

In this direction, it may be, we shall find a philosophy of miracle, of the powers of faith, of prophecy, of a human control of matter which allies exalted manhood to the creative power of God. Such an augmented power of the human soul was unquestionably taught by Jesus. As science is teaching us that hitherto men have known but little of the infinite truths of the material world, so we are beginning to find out that there are infinite possibilities in the human soul which have never been included in our philosophies.

He who enters upon the theme of the interaction of the human mind and the Divine mind, launches upon a wide and solemn sea, fathomless, shoreless, and dark, as yet. Better than Columbus sailing westward, will come Jesus to quell the wave, illumine the darkness, and reveal the shore. The human mind is the kernel ; the material world is but the shell or rind. As yet science has chiefly concerned itself with the shell. The unexplored soul is yet to be found out.

When men have gone out of the simple faith of childhood by the misinterpretation of the theory and philosophy of natural law, it ought to be to them a source of great joy and rejoicing that science itself, which misled them, has been appealed from—science not well informed, to science better informed; and that this royal doctrine, in which is so much hope, so much courage, so much rest, is returning to its place for women and children, for heroic men in straits, for all men who find themselves outside of those normal and ordinary influences upon which prosperity depends. When men are hampered and find themselves in such emergencies, if they are right-minded, if they can lift themselves higher than flesh and blood, higher than the lower forms of material law, into the communion of God, they have a right to believe that there is a divine influence, an atmospheric one, shall I call it ?—something like sunlight to the leaves and flowers; that which will lift them up and compel such laws to serve them; and, what is better, will direct them in such a way that they shall come under the influence of those laws which should give them relief.

There is one other view, however, that may supplement this, namely, that we are to take into consideration the location of this life and its relation to the life to come. As in autumn the leaves fall gently from the trees without harming the tree, externally stripped and apparently dead, whose life is yet in it, and which waits the snowy season through

for resurrection which is to come, so is it with human life.
Our seeking is often folly, and our regrets often more foolish.   We lose to gain, and gain to lose.   In short, God's
Providence is wiser than man's judgment of his own needs.
We are to bear in mind that this life is a mere planting-
time.   We are started here; we await transplantation
through resurrection, and what may seem the neglect of
God and a want of providence will reveal itself a step beyond, as being an illustrious Providence, watchful, tender,
careful.

So, brethren, be not in haste to cast away, on the instruction or the misinterpretation of science, yet crude in many
of its parts, that faith of childhood, that faith of your
fathers, that faith which is the joy and should be the courage of every right-minded man, the faith that God's eye is
on you, and that he cares, he guides, he defends, and will
bring you safely from earth to life eternal.

VII.
EVOLUTION AND THE CHURCH.

"And when he had thus spoken, he cried with a loud voice, Lazarus, come forth. And he that was dead came forth, bound hand and foot with graveclothes; and his face was bound about with a napkin. Jesus saith unto them, Loose him, and let him go."—John xi : 43, 44.

Such is the nature of the human mind and the influences that surround mankind, that no great truth ever emerges and goes forward to its demonstration and settlement, without producing among men intestine discord, divisions, controversies. Not only has Evolution been subject to this common fate of advancing truth, but it has had peculiar opposition and difficulties. Almost immediately two camps were formed, and the theistic and atheistic views divided thinkers according to their circumstances, dispositions, and previous education, as well as according to the way in which the truth struck them severally. For a long time Evolution was contested, reluctantly received, then finally embraced; but embraced by contradictory parties. The foremost thinkers of England differ from those of Germany. If we might select typical men, I should say Herbert Spencer was the typical man of English thought, and Ernst Haeckel of German or Continental thought. Both sides have taken distinct grounds. The foremost thinkers of England seem to be growing toward a spiritual center, and those of the Continent toward a material center.

The English school tend to repudiate, with growing intensity, that materialism which is accepted on the Continent and pronounce it gross and dangerous. They refuse to go

PLYMOUTH CHURCH, Sunday Morning, July 5, 1885. LESSON: Philippians ii : 1-16.

125

further at present than Agnosticism, though many of them show themselves to be impatient of camping out permanently on that ground. The ablest thinker of them all, and the ablest man that has appeared for centuries, Herbert Spencer, seems to me to have passed the winter solstice, and to be in a dawning spring and summer. Should his life be spared, I should not wonder at finding in him the ablest defender of the essential elements of a rightly interpreted Christianity that has arisen. Not that I regard every part of his system with like favor ; not that I should regard every station which he has established and position which he maintains as true or safe. Not that.—And yet, when by and by the bounds of knowledge are widened,. and the interior more perfectly surveyed and settled, I think that Herbert Spencer will be found to have given to the world more truth in one lifetime than any other man that has lived in the schools of philosophy in this world.

On the other hand, the gross materialists of the Continent, the Atheists of the Haeckel school, seem eager to detroy every vestige of religion. There is nothing in the past which they respect. They seem to be irritated if a man claims to hold on to anything in the past of a spiritual and religious nature. They look with disdain even upon Theists, and upon those that seek to find in Christianity the highest development of mankind and the ripest fruit of the doctrine of Evolution. Atheism or nothing, is their spirit; the absolute negation of any religion of former times; no compromise, no half-way station, no scrap or shred of Christianity can be permitted. And those that read them in this land, if they are unripe and have read nothing else, are very apt to catch the same feeling and say, "O, well, this preaching that Evolution is true, and attempting at the same time to hold on to the old Church and the old beliefs, is folly." Either to be a Christian in twilight, or else to be a renouncer of religion and an Atheist in sunlight, is their demand.

Now when this controversy among the Evolutionists themselves is known (and young ambitious men desirous of knowledge are reading on this subject), and when the

testimony of the newly-awakened young thinkers in their
household alarms father and mother, and when the young
and the bold in church assemblies aver the truth of Evolution, good men and good women are alarmed; they think
that everything they revere is going with a run, and they
would fain stop this defection. They think it dangerous
to encourage Evolutionary doctrines from the pulpit.

I wish, then, this morning to inquire what the result is
likely to be upon the Church and upon its ministry, of the
acceptance of the doctrine of Evolution. Is it going to tear
up the church by the roots? Is it going to destroy the pulpit? Will it overturn all those great spiritual truths on
which character has been hitherto founded? Will it turn
us over to the unkindly justice of a cold material world?
Is it to crucify afresh a living Saviour, and leave us without hope and without God in this world? Under these
vague fears, Evolution has no fair chance in the consideration of those who cling with blind affection to the old ways
and forms, and they do not give themselves any fair chance
to gain intelligent, clearer views.

Do you suppose that now, after fifty years in the Christian ministry, I could attend the funeral of religion cheerfully and joyfully, with every hereditary necessity on me,
with the whole education of my youth, with all my associations, all the endearments of my past life in my memory,
and with vivid and living sympathy with men; do you suppose that I could stand here to advocate any truth that
would destroy the substance, or in any degree materially
injure even the forms, of religion? I would die sooner!
Do you suppose from my nature and my whole example, I
could go into the course of sermons that I have preached,
and into the course of sermons that, God willing, I will
preach yet, for any other reason than that I believe that
the new view is to give to religion a power, and a scope, and
a character such as has never yet been taken and known
in the world at large? Better men than some have been, I
suppose, will never be born; better lives than certain single
lives will never appear over the horizon of time ; but that
which I look for is the change of the human race. I am not

thinking of *men*, but of *mankind.* I am not in sympathy alone with *the Church,* but with *the whole human family.* And my longing, as it has been for years, is for such teaching and such philosophies as shall lead the whole human race to a higher and a nobler condition.

Suppose, then, that Evolution should practically approve itself to be true and should be carried out as a basis of thought and teaching concerning the ways of God in his universe, will it materially affect the Church? And if so, will it be favorably or unfavorably? I say, it will, favorably. That it is going to surround the Church with alleged truths that must needs be considered, you know and I know. No great development can be made in these modern times of universal intelligence and democratic liberty, and not be felt everywhere by all men. The attempt to repress investigation, to keep out of the hands of our sons and daughters the books of the day, written by great men, full of honest and inspiring thought, expressed in lucid and attractive style, is not only wrong but impracticable. You cannot keep these books out of their hands, and it is bad to have them read by stealth. Open-faced, clear-eyed, frank, the young should be encouraged to investigate the truth; and when investigation has been permitted and has gone on, we should not allow ourselves to be terrified.

What is the Church but an association of men and women, who, by direct intercourse with God, seek to develop their moral and their spiritual nature? That is the sum and substance of it. The definition given, that the Church is a body covenanted together to worship God and maintain ordinances is, in a sense, true, but it is technical. A church has its radical idea in this, that by mutual helpfulness and by the kindling of souls together men are able to lift themselves into a higher divine life than in any other way. Some natures are so great and fruitful that they can stand alone. There are some natures that are like the Southern pine, so full of rich, fire-loving substance that they can burn of themselves and act as a torch; but the great mass of mankind need to be treated like fuel in a fireplace, stick upon stick, many and many together, that in the common heat and the common flame they may all glow. Is there anything nobler in the thought of man than the association of men and women in the purpose of living by their very highest nature? Not intellectual alone, not esthetical alone, not by gracefulness nor beauty alone, but by that which is deeper, integrity, worship, reverence, love; by spirituality, as distinguished from the mere bodily life. That is the central root-idea of the Church so far as the interior is concerned.

Now there is no absolute liberty; men feel themselves bound by forms and styles of outward worship and of inward thought. But this will perhaps be one of the achievements of Evolution,—that wherever men gather together for this supreme conception of helping each other into the higher spiritual life, they are not only the Church, but they have all the promises of the fathers and of the apostles, and the sanction of God himself. It does not need to be a church formed on any special pattern. It does not need to have such and such special forms of ordinance. It needs to have no such connections as hitherto have been accounted necessary by ecclesiastical tribunals. It inheres in the spiritual liberty of mankind to group themselves together for a higher life in God,—not only to be free from the yoke of State enactments, but from that even heavier despotism, the pressure of other men's consciences and religious prescriptions. The realization of this would be a grand ambition, a noble purpose.

But, so far as the community around about is concerned, the Church is a light and instructor; it is a school for society, an education in respect to things for which there is no other school or provisional educator. The Church is that body which undertakes to inspire and maintain conduct and character among men. There are other noble associations to produce order in society, to produce ideas of education, intellectual and philosophical. There are associations to produce wealth, associations to produce pleasure, and these, in their special allotments and offices, are not to be despised; but where else is there an institution that has come down from generation to generation,

9

having the one sole purpose of providing for the community a line of training for conduct and character? That is the peculiar mission of the Church, to take care that there is a ministry that shall form moral conduct and spiritual character in the community. The law cannot do it, the profession of the law cannot do it. Lawyers are brought mostly in contact with the unfavorable side of human nature, and they are special in their business, and there are no institutions or methods by which they could maintain in the community this idea of conduct and character. The family can do it in a measure, but the family itself will be unfit to do this, unless it is kindled by some higher intelligence than that which exists in the midst of the multitudes of ill-kept families. The medical profession can give men some knowledge of morality, which is largely connected with health, but they are in no condition to become instructors at large. The civil institutions of our land—they maintain metes and bounds, privileges and powers, but they are not instructors of this kind. The newspapers are not yet fit, quite, to be the instructors of the community as to conduct and character. They are divided among themselves; they are party "organs," that is, with liberty to throw stones at everybody but their side; or they are "independent," that is, with liberty to throw stones on either side and at everybody. But they are essentially news-vehicles, subject to sale; and they are largely influenced in their holdings-forth by the marketable value of that which they teach. This does not in the least degree diminish my regard for the value of newspapers, only it says that spiritual education is not their function. They carry out a great deal of knowledge, and they exert indirectly not a little influence for good, and they are among the signs of civilization; and in their growing excellence of a rising civilization. The newspapers of my childhood were not to be compared for excellence with those that exist to-day: but one thing is very certain, that the newspaper is not qualified at present to take charge of the conduct or the character of mankind; and the religious papers as little as any. There are multitudes of good, sound, orthodox papers that have much merit in them; but they carry the spirit of sectarianism, and the narrow, selfish, and oftentimes venomous spirit of religious contention into the household. Many of them carry also the gloom of midnight and despair with them, for how a man can say "The morning has come," who engages in promulgating the Calvinistic notions of God, I cannot conceive. There are, here and there, a very few religious papers which lay their courses on broader and more Christian lines than the sectarian charts allow; but their very fewness emphasizes the generality of the rule.

The Church, then, so far as its relation to the community is concerned, shines into every avenue of human nature; searches man not from any philosophical interest in him, but searches him for his own well-being, how to build him up into Christ Jesus. It seeks to develop the family, and is in this sense a high-priest to the priest-father and to the priest-mother. It follows men into their business, if it does its duty, and into their dealings with one another. There is the same law of truth issuing from it, and the same law of justice, and the same law of benevolence in the conduct of business as there is in the household. The Church concerns itself with the civic relations of men; and now that slavery is at an end, which once was the dominating question in our land, it necessarily lays hold on other themes of the common life and weal. In other words, it pours the light and the justice and truth and sympathy of the Gospel, not alone upon the individual or upon the family, or upon men in their business relations, but upon the whole community, seeking to bring the Divine influence to bear upon men in their widest combinations. It embosoms, finally, the whole world. It has taken for its motto "The field is the world," and given a new glory to the old pagan declaration, "Whatever concerns man concerns me."

Now, is there no need of such an institution? If the Church should be destroyed, would not there be a want felt that would reconstruct the Church? If you were to obliterate from the Christian world the churches that now exist, the necessities of human nature would bring them to

life again, perhaps purified, simplified, made more useful.
There is no Evolutionary doctrine that can take away from
human nature the necessity of the institution which concerns
itself in developing mankind from the low to the intermediate, and from the intermediate to the higher stages.

What changes will perhaps be made by Evolution? Well,
I suppose if it will not give a circumscription or reduction
of the externals of the Church, it certainly will put them in
a different light from that which they have hitherto had.
I think the time will come very soon when the central consideration in the Church will be spirituality in men. At
present we have not risen to that height; at present we
are a great way from it. A truly noble, personally
pure, just and upright man, in sympathy with all his
fellow-men, who does not avow the doctrines of the Church,
and has not passed through its regimental ordeal, is considered yet, by the great multitude of religionists in
the Christian world, as an outsider. He may be a model
of all that Christ would have in a man, but if his views
of Church organization, of worship, of ordinances, and
then of theoretical doctrines, do not agree with the professional views of the Church itself, he is not admitted,
or is shut out. Children look upon him with wonder,
and marvel whether it is possible that such a man, who
does not believe in the Church, will go to heaven. The
day is coming when the spiritual character will dominate
everything else, and will be the evidence for which a man
will be courted and brought into Church concord ; and
when such a day as that comes, I do not believe that
the Unitarian and Universalist Sunday-schools of Brooklyn
will be excluded from the Orthodox ranks in the parade
on our Saint Children's Day. I cannot help feeling, I will
not say indignation, but a pity that does not stand far from
contempt, for those miserable, squabbling, sectarian men
that visit not the sins of the fathers but the sins of the cate-
chism upon the children, and refuse the little ones of all
the different denominations the right to come together and
love one another, and triumph with each other in the march.
But if any man has children that are so exceedingly weak

that they are liable to catch heresy by contact in the street, I think he had better keep them at home on that day; indeed, why should they be allowed to associate with the little heretics at all—at day-school, at play, in their little social parties ! The fact that these more intimate associa- tions are constantly permitted shows the senseless folly (to put it mildly) of the ecclesiastical exclusion.

There will also be a cure of the despotism of the Church and its conceit, as if God had given some special deposit of the truth to each particular Church or denomination which they were bound to care for, and which none other had. No safety out of the Church, no covenanted safety for an unbaptized child ! These are the faultings of a pass- ing age ; past, perhaps. No grace except through the Church, as if the sun did not shine on the good and the bad, and the rain did not fall on the just and on the unjust; no grace that comes to a man of his own choice and en- deavor, none that does not come from the ordinance and through the priest that administers it; a monopoly of God's Spirit in the hands of men in Church connection. I think these things will be exploded, and the Church will be all the better to have them exploded. There will also be more and more, with the passing away of these despotic claims and dispositions and tendencies, a gradual cure of Church quarrelsomeness. One of the saddest effects in connection with the institutions of Christianity—not Christianity itself —has been that the line of their march has been a line of skulls and bones and blood, and the music of their prog- ress has been sighs and weepings and sorrows. It has been clashing, quarreling, fighting; for let me tell you, that when the battle is set upon the conscience, there is no such battle as that known in this whole world. Let a body of men think that God has inspired them above everybody else—nay, laid on them the duty to declare and call men to believe certain things ; and let another body be called at just the opposite side, both of them called of God, both of them raising big conscience, both of them defending the faith that was given to the saints, and history shows that there is no such quarrelsomeness on the face of the earth.

Conscience is a good thing, conscience in love; but conscience in hate is the very devil of ecclesiasticism.

All this is being done; that is to say, the Church is experiencing the gradual ameliorations and changes which are in the air, as one may say, certainly which are in the providence of God. There is a growing tendency to unity in the Church; it has not yet overcome, by any means, the spirit of contention, but unexpectedly the work of Christian men outside of their churches is drawing them together inside of their churches. You bring together the Protestants and the Catholics, and all the Protestants of two hundred or more sectaries that have a special doctrine or special form or special ordinance, or special something, and they enter together the field of temperance, they work together with some great patriotic enthusiasm, or they are touched with the sufferings of races unseen, far away—deluges, earthquakes, famines, diseases, pestilences that waste them; they come together in public meetings and discuss these questions. What a surprise it is for a Protestant to find that the Catholic pastor has neither hoofs nor horns, that he is a man after all, and a good man! And I know not but that the same wonder exists among our Catholic brethren who find a robust faith and a cheerful piety in men that do not belong to their Church. At any rate, the bringing together of churchmen, outside of their church connections, is civilizing them; and I hope yet to see the day when that proverb will have died out of the memory of man: "I know they are Christians, they quarrel so."

Perhaps as yet the unity of the Church is growing by the interior rather than by the exterior. Asceticism is also dying out. The great world movement that is going on, and of which the Evolutionary philosophy is but one of the stages and signs, is really changing the dispositional orthodoxies of churches. I think every man will be a witness that, with the exception of here and there a remote corner (where the mail does not come but once a month), into the churches of our land that take the newspapers and read what God is thinking and doing all over the world, there is creeping in a spirit of hope and of cheerfulness. Caution is being humbled. Boldness is coming to the cheer of trust and of love. Theology is not half so black-faced as it was. Men apologize now for preaching doctrines which once they preached with all the thunder of the old prophets, as they supposed. The whole aspect of religion as it is being developed from pulpit to pulpit, is more hopeful, more joyful, more loving, more genial, humane and sympathetic. It is a change very greatly to advantage.

Then, too, in connection with this, there is growing in the Church a specialization in the direction of amusement. Why, in my boyhood I was forbidden to walk in the garden on Sunday, unless I was going to fodder the cow and the horse (which were never so well taken care of as on that blessed day!). But whether we might write a letter on Sunday was a grave question; it brought into serious doubt "the evidences" of many persons that were church-members. To ride out on Sunday was deadly heresy. Now, religion has itself developed the spirit of enjoyment, and is getting rid of the old ascetic side that believed that the business of the Christian was to be unhappy here with the hope of being happier in heaven. That ascetic soot that went through the flues of the Church is being swept out. Entertainments are being given in the churches. This very platform has seen things which would have made John Knox shiver. To see a Sunday-school picnic would have made John Calvin run, crying, "Horror, horror!" But the Church itself is the parent of amusement now, and has said sensibly to itself, "If our children, according to the growing public sentiment, must enjoy themselves, we must be present, and see to it that they have not only amusement, but under the best circumstances." The change is steadily going on. It is a specialization of the functions of the Church to give to those that need it, the young and the overladen, the replenishment of joy and of happiness. Thus happily the Church is doing things that were unheard of in other days. There used to be assemblages of ministers, diets, councils, when venerable men, many of whom ought to have been in State's prison, came together to determine what was for the best interests of the Church, and corrupted the cities in which they held their sessions, as in the Council of Trent. There used to be enough of the associations and assemblies of the officers of the Church; but now the Church, in its whole body, laymen and all, has its meetings. They are beginning to have their councils, their summer meetings at Chautauqua, their Ocean Grove and Wesley Park meetings—they are beginning to have home courses of reading for the year laid out. Thus the Church is not simply attempting to act within its own walls, but is seeking to spread the spirit of progress, of purity in thought, in refinement and enjoyment. These things are buds that have sprung out of the boughs of the old Church life, and they are increasing every decade in number, in sweetness, and in promise of a blessed fruit. The camp-meetings may be said to have been the type, the beginning; but even these are changing; and in imitation of these or upon their suggestion, other, and variously conducted associations are carried on under the care of the Church in every denomination in this land. With all its faults, is there anything that aims so high as the Church; is there any other thing that could fill the void if it should sink?

But then is there anything in Evolution that would desire to destroy the Church? Is not this influence in the Church itself one of the signs of the diversified unfolding of God's plans on the earth going to show the truthfulness of that philosophy of God's methods which modern philosophers have named Evolution, one of the results of that Providence that inspires growth upon growth, and growth upon growth? Nay more,—and this is the point,—I firmly believe that the acceptance of this doctrine, which seems to me inevitable, is to be one of God's most effective instruments in intensifying and hastening the progress of these and similar blessed changes. In short, *Evolution will affect the Church*, but for its greater health and power among men.

Then, next, is there any danger that the Pulpit and preaching will be injuriously affected by the progress of Evolution? One would think, from the vehemence and zeal with which the pulpit sometimes preaches against

Evolution, that it was afraid itself of being extinguished. That it will in some respects be changed and bettered, I cannot doubt; but the function itself is divine, and it is necessary to the human race. It walks with the progress of God in the whole evolutionary scheme.

The ideal of the preacher is, a large nature filled with enthusiasm for God, but even more for man, and caring for men as the chief care of his own life more than for the Church, more than for the law, more than for theology. A true preacher is a man that lives for his fellow-men, caring for them as a mother cares for her babes. The whole world may go whirling round and round the mother's head, but there is only one center to her life—the babe in her lap. The man of God, called for the sake of saving his fellow-men, must live in that as the chief end of his existence. Is there any priest or pontifex, or any other ordained officer that ever was known among men, who stands as high as this ideal of the simple man, fired with the love of God and the love of his fellow-men, giving himself voluntarily to their service? Is a man, of stature so grand as this, to be overthrown by the philosophy of Evolution? It is to make just such men that evolution is striving, exhibiting the force of soul on soul. Centuries have been changed by the power of a single man. The whole course of history has been changed by the vital force that lies in one single will. As the live sparks from the hunter's pipe, thrown carelessly into the ripe grass of the prairie, will kindle a flame that sweeps over leagues and leagues, so one single glowing coal of a man has burned over a superstitious age and changed the whole aspect of humanity. And if there be multiplied men, ordained of God and not of their fellow-men, inspired by divine zeal to work for the welfare of their fellow-men,—men who have that as their ambition, as their occupation, as their pride, as their joy, as their light and reward forever, and whose motto is, "Not yours, but you;" is there any conception of vocation that is grander than that? If you put purple on him and a tiara, and give him a pontifical scepter, why should we think him any worse? He is certainly not any better. The force of a holy life and a Christ-like disposition can remove mountains. I have seen a great many pictures of Christ, but I never yet saw him on an earthly throne or with an earthly crown upon his head, except that of thorns. The Christ of Art was one made sorrowful by self-sacrifice; the Christ of the Gospel exhibits the triumph and joy of self-sacrifice. For the joy that was set before him, he endured the cross and despised the shame, he lived among people as one of them, their sorrows touched him, he went to them, not waiting their approach to his dignity and his grandeur, but, like the sun, spreading himself wherever he went in light and warmth and heat. That is the idea of the true ministry; not of a secular ministry, not of a man called by routine, not of a man who simply regards the Church as an honorable profession and accepts its liturgy and its method, and takes care of them just as an engineer takes care of a machine, or as a janitor takes care of a great building. The man of God is moved by the same impulse that moves God and the eternities. Is there any conception of manhood that is grander than that? Can the world spare such men? It may chide the men who pretend to be such, for their delinquencies. It may demand that men serving God in the way of serving the people shall be what they profess to be; but Evolution is not going to take away from the grandeur of the idea, or the necessity of it in the history of the human race.

In sympathy with all God's going-on in earth, in society, the preacher is to be, and not a mere lecturer. The Christian ministry steadily develops the unsensuous imagination of men, for faith is in large degree imagination; and the calling of men from week to week to think of that which is not visible, to think of that which is supersensuous, to think of endless spaces and durations, lifting them above the to-day and the present physical organization, lifting them into the invisible sphere, and that through days and months and years, and scores of years—is not this a prodigious education to the imagination and the faith, and the supersensuous part of mankind? It is so powerful that it may carry with it a hundred unnecessary ceremonies and baggages. The steady lifting up of men into the conscious atmosphere of God, the steady work of giving men a higher standpoint, and a better ground from which to judge men and things, and from which to create standards of morality and spirituality before their congregations—is there nothing in that? There has been a sharp distinction made between morality and piety, and there is a difference; but it is just the difference between the unripe and the ripe. Morality is the beginning of spirituality. No spiritual element ever existed without a foundation of morality. I have just been beholding with fresh delight the achievements of the magnolia, which in spring carries at its very top the bright white cup, as if it were filled with the very ether and essence of sunlight and fragrance. And yet that cup, holding itself so, is dependent on that homely, dirt-colored root at the bottom. Destroy the root and you will destroy the cup. All the way from the bottom clear up to the top there is this perfect unity of organization and evolvement, and as the sweet censer of fragrance and beauty in the tree is intimately connected with its root, so morality and spirituality are one, only at different stages and positions of growth.

Then, the distinction between natural and revealed religion will be abolished. They are both one. Natural religion has nothing in it that is not of God, and revealed religion has God in it. It is simply one God, who speaks by creation outward and by creation inward; these throw light on each other and help each other, and together give man the most perfect view of divine nature. Evolution will not take away the unity of interpretation of God in Nature and God in the Word, but will give more power to each of them. And, above all, Evolution is going to drive out of the world the Manichean doctrine, the idea that man was cursed in the fall of a fabulous ancestor, that that fall corrupted his very body, blood, and bones, that a man inherits the corruption, and that the flesh is corrupt in and of itself. This wild heathenism, this outrageous paganism, is lurking in the blood of the Church yet, but will be purged away by Evolution. Thus, the minister will keep exalting morality into spirituality evermore, for morality is the root of which spirituality is the blossom and the fruit; ceaselessly calling men to note their imperfections, to slay sin, to cut it up by the roots, to humble themselves before God, to repent of sins, to begin a higher life, and to carry on that higher life yet higher and higher. Is that an element in society that can be dispensed with? Great as is knowledge, great as is true science, they will always continue to be mere Intellect, which never arouses the whole man. It is only the truth as it is in Christ Jesus that rakes a man fore and aft, that attacks him from bottom to top, that gives to his whole nature,—physical, social, moral, and spiritual,—the food that it needs, and which is indispensably connected with the unfolding of man into a perfect creature in Christ Jesus. A lecturer, a mere dealer in pure thought, may be in his own sphere and place desirable, as certainly he is; but a minister who is merely a scientific professor is no minister of the Gospel.

Then there will be other changes that will make the pulpit not simply necessary, but far more powerful than it has ever been. I believe that there is rising upon the world, to shine out in wonderful effulgence, a view of God as revealed in the history of the unfolding creation that men will not willingly let die—partly through a better understanding of the nature of God in Christ Jesus, and partly also through a growing knowledge of the universal God, the all-present God, the spiritual God, pervading time and space and eternity. The frowning God, the partial God, the Fate-God, men would fain let die; but the Father-God, watching, caring, bearing burdens, whose very life it is to take care of life and bring it up from stage to stage—that thought of God will quench utterly the lurid light of Atheism. We are coming to a time when we shall be so assailed by Atheistic philosophy, that men will be forced back upon this nobler view of God; and so, indirectly, God will restrain the wrath of men, and cause the remainder thereof to praise him.

Thus the Church will leave behind many of the things that have rather hindered than helped it on the road, as it has done already. Where, to-day, is the controversy on *filioque*, or the generation of the Son? Where is the great doctrine that has almost caused saints to swear at each other, as to the eternal generation of Christ? Where are the controversies that filled the land in regard to natural ability and moral inability, or *vice versa?* Where are the controversies touching transubstantiation that have deluged nations in blood—where are they all? If one would know anything about them, he must hunt in history and obscure places. They are dropped. There are a great many other things that theology will drop. That is all,—drop; and be all the more powerful for that which it lacks. The doctrine of original sin will disappear. We need not be afraid of getting rid of original sin, because we can get all the actual transgression that the world needs to take its place. The eternity of conscious suffering, in connection with that extraordinary and incomprehensible apparent waste that has been going on in the human family from the earliest day, must go. You must either take away the fatherhood from God, or you must take away that horrible doctrine from theology. The doctrines of foreordination, and election, and decrees, as hitherto taught, may become beautiful, like old castles when they are no longer inhabited, and when vines and ivy have grown all over them. They may have historical value for their associations, but they will very rapidly empty churches that continue to preach them. The moral sentiment of the people has advanced so far that they cannot bear the old theology. The atonement confounded with the fable of Adam's fall will give place to a more glorious development of the outcoming of God's nature in the fullness of time, and the moral power that streams from the face of God in Christ Jesus.

The Bible will be a re-living book, not as it is handed to us, petrified by interpretations from the scholastic point of view, but as food, eatable, digestible, and useful. In other words, the Bible will be taught just as now it is used. Men know perfectly well, when they use the Bible as their spiritual guide, what part to select. They select the things that they need, the things that stir them, the things that their moral consciousness adopts.   They know the different value between the long genealogical chapters in Chronicles and the Gospels of John and of Matthew.   They know that there is a different weight and value to different parts of the Bible, a volume of sixty-six different books, in different languages, published in different ages, with a thousand years between some of them, representing the lyrics and the literature, all the legislation, all the great judicatories, and the slender stock of medical knowledge, of the Jewish race.   That volume, put together in such a way, is not of uniform value in all parts.   The doctrine of inspiration which teaches us that God wrote it and the whole of it right straight through, men do not believe, nor will they now fight for it.   Ministers may assert it officially in the pulpit, but they do not personally believe it. Their own uses of it, their own experiences of it, their personal familiarity with the Word of God, as God's food for the soul, teaches them the truth in fact that ought to be taught in theory, and that will make the Word of God a thousand times more effective.

Enough of this—for let who will look upon every part of organized Christianity as it exists now, and he will see the changes that are taking place.   But they will be gradual. That is right.   They will help man.   They will give men's minds time to accommodate themselves to changing views. Simply to hold views of fundamental moral principles is one thing; holding these views of moral principles organized into a physical institution is another thing.   Men of Babylonish genius are still crying to the young and thoughtful, "Search for the old paths."   Yes, those as old as God !   It is the old paths of man's making that may well be relocated.   To search for the old paths is against the practice of the modern engineer, who seeks to lay out the road on a straight line.   The old paths used to run round and round, up and down, through swamps and quagmires, and over almost impassable hills; yet when at last the best path is struck straight through between the two great cities, the croakers say, "Search for the old paths."   That which is true of physics is truer yet of morality and religion. Theology and the Church are undergoing a process of evolution, towards perfection, changing upwards and for the better. Those elements that are changing the other way are gradually approaching dissolution, for destruction and evolution are twins. They work together. In the history of God's creation, things that are not good, or that are too weak to live, perish right alongside of things that are stronger and better adapted. Deterioration and destruction are part and parcel of the great process of evolution going on all the time. The presumption of Evolution is adverse to the claims of authority both in the Church and in the State. You know what the history of civil liberty has been. Nothing has been accounted to be so dangerous and so disastrous to man as the liberty of the individual. At every stage of unfolding from the beginning down to the commonwealth of America, all philosophers almost, and all potentates, have resisted this wild fanaticism of democracy. It is not safe, they say, to trust men by themselves; and the danger of trusting men by themselves in commonwealths has been the theme of ages. Alongside that has been the cry of churches with aristocratic ministries and ponderous governments—the cry of "Authority;" it will not do to let men think for themselves. It will not do to leave men in democratic Christian conditions in regard to what they believe. You must have ordained men and ordained customs, and ordinances fixed of God. The same liturgy of folly that ran through the civil progress of the world has been running also through the ecclesiastical and the theological. In both one and the other, experiment will show that under the great canopy of God's providence men as they grow in intelligence are safer the more you give them liberty. Their dissuasions and dissensions and such elements are preparatory to a new coadhesion. Pruning makes more fruit, not less, in every vine and in every fruit-tree; and so it is in the Church.

At last I come back to my text, and I seem to myself to see the Church bound, entombed, hearing the voice of Him that stood without, crying, "Lazarus, come forth!" and out of the tomb and out of the crypt, staggering, half-blind, he emerges; bound about with grave-clothes, and with a napkin round about his face. Out of all antiquity, out of all synods, out of all councils, out of all ecclesiastical hierarchies, out of every form of entombment, out of all bondages, the Church comes. And methinks I hear the Voice of the living Christ calling out from heaven to-day, "Loose him; let him go!"

Young men, that wait upon my ministry, I do not say to you, lay aside the dangerous books of modern thought; I say, read them. Do not be afraid of them, do not be afraid of change. But do not make haste; do not be misguided by false lights. I am for liberty of knowledge, for liberty in philosophy, in spite of organization and precedents and of all that is past. Go on from ignorance to twilight, and from twilight to sunrise, and from sunrise to mid-day. But be sure of one thing: whatever philosophy has taught or is teaching, be sure of one thing—you are a sinful and imperfect man, and that is the root-truth for you. And again: God is abroad in the world to give inspiration and help to you, and to lift you up out of your animal life into spiritual. These two truths are to be held as you hold your very birthright of life itself. You are sinners; and God, through Jesus Christ, has come into the world to save sinners. Be lifted then into communion and intercourse and likeness with God. Read on; fill your mind with facts and ideas, but do not be in haste to give up the covenants of your fathers. Do not be skeptical of the reality of piety. Is there no mother that rises from the horizon of your memory to tell you that her religion was true—not its doctrines, but its substance? Is there no venerable patriarch remembered as your father, whose justice and charity and truth were such that you can say, "If ever there was a Christian he was one"? You have seen what religion is in actual disposition and in actual life. Hold on to that substance. You are a dying man with but one life to live and with one great hope. If you would uncover it and look it in the face, and hope on, and live again in a better sphere, and under nobler culture, see to it that no raw knowledge and no yet green information shall replace in your soul that central substance. Say to yourself: " I am of the dust; I am brother of the worm; I am companion of the beast. But I am rising steadily away from them. I go up toward inspiration and light, yet half-clouded; I feel in me that I am of God and am a son of God, and I will not give up my birthright, neither for the bait of pleasure, neither for the bribe of power and ambition, neither for the cry of the multitude."

The verities which can never be overturned are those which are set down in the Bible as the unchangeable and everlasting truths of Revelation:

"*And now abideth Faith, Hope, Love, these three; but the greatest of these is Love*" (1 Cor. xiii : 13).

" *The fruit of the Spirit is Love, Joy, Peace, Longsuffering, Gentleness, Goodness, Faith, Meekness, Self-control : against such there is no law*" (Gal. v : 22, 23).

"*Love is of God; and every one that loveth is born of God, and knoweth God. He that loveth not, knoweth not God;* FOR GOD IS LOVE" (1 John iv : 7, 8).

10

For EU product safety concerns, contact us at Calle de José Abascal, 56–1°,
28003 Madrid, Spain or eugpsr@cambridge.org.

www.ingramcontent.com/pod-product-compliance
Ingram Content Group UK Ltd.
Pitfield, Milton Keynes, MK11 3LW, UK
UKHW020324140625
459647UK00018B/2005